SEA HARRIER AND AV-8B

SEA HARRIER AND AV-8B

ROBERT JACKSON

BLANDFORD

First published in the UK 1989 by Blandford Press,
Artillery House, Artillery Row, London SW1P 1RT

Copyright © 1989 Robert Jackson

Distributed in the United States by
Sterling Publishing Co. Inc.,
2 Park Avenue, New York NY 10016

Distributed in Australia by
Capricorn Link (Australia) Pty. Ltd.,
P.O. Box 665, Lane Cove, NSW 2066

British Library Cataloguing in Publication Data
Jackson, Robert, *1941–*
    British Aerospace Sea Harrier and McDonnell
    Douglas AV-8.—(Weapons and warfare).
    1. Harrier (Jet fighter plane)
    I. Title II. Series
    623.74'6407   UG1242.F5

Typeset by Ronset Typesetters Ltd, Darwen, Lancs.
Printed in Great Britain by The Bath Press, Avon.

Frontispiece
Sea Harriers of No. 801
Squadron, HMS *Invincible*,
during the latter's visit
to Australia in 1983.

CONTENTS

PREFACE

On Monday 8 February 1988, former Hawker Chief Test Pilot A. W. 'Bill' Bedford landed aboard the aircraft carrier HMS *Ark Royal* in a Sea Harrier T.4N of 899 Naval Air Squadron, piloted by Lieutenant Alistair McLaren. Accompanying the T.4N was a Sea Harrier FRS.1 flown by 899's commanding officer, Commander Scott Lidbetter.

Twenty-five years earlier, at about midday on 8 February 1963, Bill Bedford became the first pilot in history to land a V/STOL aircraft on the deck of an aircraft carrier, touching down on the deck of the previous *Ark Royal* off Lyme Bay near Portland in Hawker P.1127 XP831, the ancestor of the Harrier and Sea Harrier.

Between these two events, separated by a quarter of a century, is the story of a remarkable and revolutionary aircraft. This book tells that story in full. It records the evolution of a weapons system, from the Royal Navy's basic operational requirement, through the Sea Harrier FRS.1, to the next generation, the FRS.2, and looks even beyond that to the possibility of a supersonic derivative for the future. It tells how the designers have overcome one technical hurdle after another and, in parallel with the Royal Navy's needs, developed techniques that have boosted the aircraft's operational effectiveness – and of how the United States Marine Corps developed new tactical applications for the AV-8A and B, some of which have re-crossed the Atlantic to be used by the British services.

ACKNOWLEDGEMENTS

Many people have assisted with the preparation of this book. Above all, I am indebted to British Aerospace's Military Aircraft Division at Kingston for permission to draw on company material and use copyright photographs – and in particular to John S. Godden of the Public Relations Department, who collaborated with me throughout and whose unflagging enthusiasm for the Sea Harrier was reflected in his constant willingness to help. I am grateful, too, for the help of the Photographic Section staff at Kingston for processing the necessary material, and to Alan Todd for delving into his copious files to unearth obscure items of Sea Harrier information. Special thanks are also due to Angela Tunstall, who spent a great deal of time typing, proof-reading and indexing the work. All uncredited photographs are the copyright of British Aerospace.

Robert Jackson

1 BRITISH V/STOL

The story of the vertical take-off application to air combat really begins in 1945, when Germany made plans to mass-produce a rocket-powered target defence interceptor, the Bachem Ba 349 Natter (Viper). The idea was that the Natter would be launched vertically from a ramp by four rocket boosters and would then climb to an altitude of about seven and a half miles under the power of its main motor. After attacking the target with its nose-mounted battery of 73mm rockets, the pilot would pull a lever, detaching the nose section; another lever deployed a drogue parachute attached to the rear of the aircraft; and the sudden deceleration was supposed to eject the pilot, who would then make a normal parachute descent. However, the only manned test flight ended in disaster: the Natter dived into the ground only seconds after launch, killing its pilot.

Other wartime German VTOL (vertical take-off and landing) projects, which never left the drawing board, included the Focke-Achgelis Fa 269 carrier-based fighter that was designed to use thrust vectoring – a single BMW radial engine in the fuselage driving two large-diameter propellers aft of the wing, which could be rotated downwards to provide vertical thrust and rearwards for horizontal flight – and the Focke-Wulf Triebflügel, a jet-powered cole-opter fighter project. The Triebflügel's small jets were mounted at the end of three long arms which, in turn, were mounted at about the mid-section of the aircraft's fuselage, the idea being that when the arms rotated they would act like a helicopter's rotor blades and lift the device, which sat on its tail.

The main problem confronting designers researching the vertical take-off concept was to find a foolproof means of ensuring stability during the critical transition phase between vertical and horizontal flight. However, in 1951, when the US Navy issued a requirement for a small fighter aircraft capable of operating from platforms on merchant ships for convoy protection, Convair and Lockheed both launched into a research programme that was to produce surprising long-term results. Each company developed an aircraft of roughly similar configuration, a 'tail-sitter' using a powerful turboprop engine with large contra-rotating propellers to eliminate torque. The aircraft, using a simple, two-axis auto-stabilizer, would be flown vertically off the ground and then bunted over into horizontal flight; during landing it would hang on its propellers, which would then perform the same function as a helicopter's rotor and lower it to a landing on its tail castors. Both aircraft, the Lockheed XFV-1 and the Convair XFY-1, flew in 1954. The XFY-1 was the more successful design and underwent a comprehensive flight test programme, but in 1956 the US Navy withdrew its requirement and abandoned VTOL research. The reasons given were technical ones, such as instability during the transition phase, but the real reason was that a powerful lobby of senior officers in the US Navy saw the development of the VTOL concept as a threat to the production of newer and larger aircraft carriers. It was to be many years before the VTOL concept returned to the US Navy as an operational reality, through American interest in the Harrier.

In the United Kingdom, practical experiments based on the VTOL concept began in 1953 with the first vertical flight trials of the Rolls-Royce Thrust Measuring Rig. Known more popularly as 'The Flying Bedstead', it had two Rolls-Royce Nene turbojets installed horizontally at opposite ends of the assembly, their tailpipes directed vertically downwards near the mass centre. While these trials were in progress, the Ministry of Supply issued Specification ER.143 for a research aircraft which could take off vertically by jet-lift and then accelerate forward into normal cruising flight. The thinking behind this specification was that VTOL might have an application in the design of future transport aircraft rather than in combat aircraft designs; the same train of thought was also being followed in the United States and resulted in VTOL research types such as the Lockheed Model 330 Humming Bird, which was built as part of the US Army Transportation Research Command Program.

The design submitted by Short Brothers, the PD.11 – a small tailless delta aircraft with five RB.108 engines, four for lift and one for forward propulsion – was judged to be the most promising, and in August 1954 Shorts received a contract to build two prototypes, under the designation Short SC.1.

The first SC.1, XG900, was initially not fitted with lift engines and made a conventional maiden flight on 2 April 1957; it was the second prototype, XG905, which began tethered hovering trials in May 1958. On 6 April 1960, at the Royal Aeronautical Establishment (RAE) at Bedford, test pilot Tom Brooke-Smith achieved the first complete transition from level flight to vertical descent and vertical climb, following a conventional take-off. That summer, XG900 now having had its battery of lift engines fitted, both SC.1s developed short, rolling take-off techniques from unprepared surfaces, the objects of which were to avoid ground erosion

and to allow flights at increased take-off weights.

In April 1961 XG900 was handed over to RAE Bedford, while XG905 went to Belfast to be fitted with a new auto-stabilization system, designed to compensate for gusts. More than 80 flights were made with the new system, starting in June 1963. The development pilot was J. R. Green, who had joined Shorts from the RAE. On 2 October, Green was returning to land when the gyros failed, producing false references which caused the auto-stabilizer to fly the aircraft into the ground. The failure occurred at an altitude of less than 30ft, giving Green no time to revert to manual control. XG905 hit the ground upside down and Green was killed. The aircraft itself was repaired and flew again in 1966, carrying out trials with the Blind Landing Experimental Unit.

At no time was the Short SC.1 intended to lead to the development of a more advanced

Pegasus gas flows, 1958 onwards, and (far right) the 9,000lb Pegasus 1.

combat aircraft: indeed, when the SC.1 began its trials in 1958 the Air Ministry was showing little or no interest in the concept, the general feeling being that the use of four or five engines solely to provide lift would result in a prohibitive weight penalty. What was needed was a different solution – and it came from an unexpected source.

THE BE53 PEGASUS ENGINE

In 1956 Michel Wibault, a French engineer, approached Bristol Aero Engines (now part of Rolls-Royce) with a proposal for a short take-off and landing (STOL) aircraft in which the thrust could be moved through an arc or 'vectored' from horizontally rearward to vertically downward. The power unit for Wibault's 'Ground Attack Gyropter' consisted of an 800hp Bristol Orion turboprop driving four centrifugal blowers, the exhaust casings of which could be rotated to direct the jet of compressed air, and hence the reaction, or thrust, through 90°. Although the Gyropter was too heavy to be practical, the concept of thrust vectoring – being able to direct all the thrust from the horizontal to the vertical and at any angle in between – had many practical advantages over the thrust deflection devices under investigation at that time.

Following engineering studies at Bristol, the thrust vectoring idea was developed into the first BE53 configuration of 1957, using the Orpheus jet engine as a central power generator. It was this form of the BE53 that was first studied by the Hawker design team at Kingston. Since only part of this engine's thrust output could be vectored, it did not provide a satisfactory basis for a useful V/STOL military aircraft. However, research discussions between the aircraft and engine design teams rapidly resulted in the BE53 configuration being changed in order to make the concept more adaptable to a practical V/STOL fighter.

Within about a year of the P.1127 V/STOL studies starting at Kingston, the engine had evolved considerably, with four principal changes. First, a common air intake for the fan and high-pressure (HP) compressors had been introduced, the fan thus supercharging the HP spool; second, contra-rotation of the two shafts had been introduced to minimize gyroscopic coupling forces; third, the turbine discharge had been split to give two further swivel nozzles, thus allowing all the engine's thrust to be vectored; and fourth, the use of compact, cascaded nozzles at all four outlets in lieu of the original large-radius bent pipes reduced external drag and swivelling torque. The last three of these changes came about directly as a result of ideas and pressure from the aircraft team. The engine was named Pegasus, after the inspiration of poetry, or the winged horse of the Muses.

It was in this form that the engine first ran, in September 1959, at 9,000lb thrust. However, a decision to use HP instead of low-pressure (LP) air for aircraft control forces in V/STOL flight demanded the use of a higher mass flow compressor. Thus modified, the Pegasus 2, of 11,000lb thrust, ran in February 1960, and was cleared for flight in the prototype P.1127 in the late summer of that year. Since that time, almost every component in the engine had been changed, but the thermodynamic and mechanical principles of the Pegasus have remained unaltered for over thirty years.

The Pegasus is a simple, robust and reliable two-shaft turbofan. Thrust is produced from

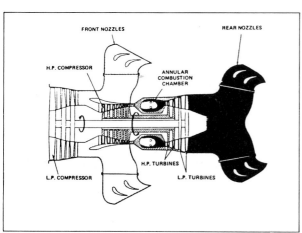

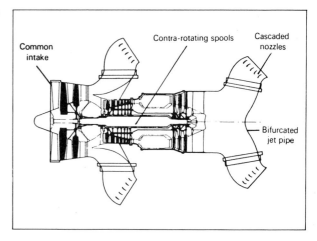

four separate nozzles which can be rotated through 100°, from fully aft to about 10° forward of vertical. It has a bypass ratio of 4.3:1 in V/STOL, and the total airflow is about 430lb/sec, over 60 per cent of which is exhausted through the front nozzles; airflow conditions at the front jets are about 1,200fs and 110°C and at the rear jets about 1,800fs and 670°C. The engine has two compressor/turbine systems, which contra-rotate in order to eliminate gyroscopic forces in V/STOL flight. The fan compression ratio is 2.4:1 and the overall compression ratio almost 15:1. The Pegasus has an installed thrust-to-weight ratio of nearly 6:1, among the highest for non-afterburning engines.

THE P.1127

By the end of 1958, the first flight configuration of the P.1127 was defined, and early in 1959 drawing issue for manufacture commenced using company funds. Although 75 per cent of the funding for the engine was supplied by the US Government through the Mutual Weapons Development Agency in Paris, no service sponsor could be found for the aircraft. The British Government finally decided to support the aircraft and funding was authorized in early 1960 when the first prototype was about half complete.

Two Pegasus 2-powered P.1127 prototypes were built, XP831 and XP836, first taking to the air on 21 October 1960 and 7 July 1961 respectively. Although the form, content and performance of the vehicle and its systems have been considerably changed and improved, all the features of the Harrier were present in the first demonstrator and almost all the seeds of the Harrier's future can be identified in these historic aircraft.

The first hovers took place in October 1960 and first conventional flights in March 1961; transitions to and from wingborne flight were accomplished in September 1961 and, in December 1961, the P.1127 became the world's first V/STOL jet aircraft to go supersonic in a dive. A development batch (DB) of four aircraft followed, XP972, XP976, XP980, and XP984, the last three powered by the Pegasus 3. The first DB aircraft, XP972, flew on 5 April 1962, and the last, XP984, on 13 February 1964.

SUPERSONIC V/STOL

Hawker did not consider that the subsonic development was the ultimate V/STOL aircraft,

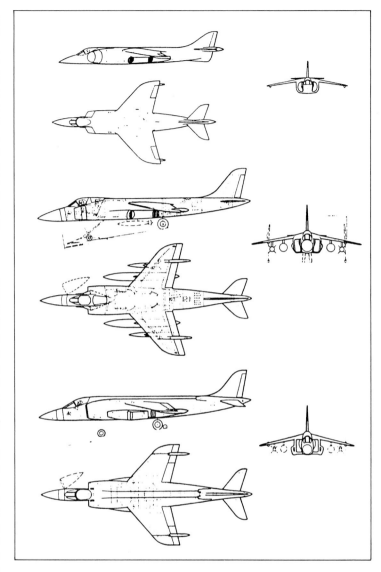

and studies had already been underway of a supersonic V/STOL aircraft, the P.1150, from which the P.1154 design emerged: using the same configuration and a vectored thrust Pegasus with plenum chamber burning (PCB), it looked like a stretched and refined P.1127. Plenum chamber burning involves the combustion of fuel in fully oxygen-rich air and at higher pressures than in most reheat systems, and the ability to obtain and sustain PCB is remarkably good compared to the reheat systems in conventional engines. The combustors, known as collanders, are located in the plenum chamber outlet ducts of the front nozzles and use a fuel manifold and ignition system similar to that of a reheat unit. Using the

The P.1150, predecessor
to the P.1154 (top); the
P.1154 AW406 RN two-
seat supersonic interceptor
strike aircraft of 1962,
powered by a BS.100/9
vectored thrust turbofan
with PCB (centre); and the
P.1154/2 Joint Service
ground attack/all weather
interceptor of 1963
(bottom).

Pegasus 5 engine with PCB, it was estimated that the P.1150 would reach Mach 1.7 – a substantial advance. However, the P.1150 design was fairly quickly overtaken by events.

The NATO Basic Military Requirement No. 3 competition of 1961 called for a supersonic V/STOL attack fighter, and it was the P.1154 proposal that emerged as the technical first choice of the multi-nation assessment team, sharing overall first place with the Mirage IIIV. However, NATO had no procurement resources and could only make their choice known to the member nations. Nevertheless, the Royal Air Force and the Royal Navy, in the knowledge that the successful NBMR3 design was likely to become the standard NATO strike/attack aircraft, wrote separate Operational Requirements around the P.1154, and further project studies went ahead at Kingston from 1962. The programme quickly became embroiled in inter-service and political wrangles and a complex of conflicting demands.

ROYAL NAVY INTEREST

The first substantial reference to the potential of operating V/STOL fighters from ships had been made in a 1959 Hawker P.1127 document that bore a 'Secret' classification. This summarized, in eloquent prose, the anticipated operational benefits and flexibility of V/STOL deck flying, although there was little in it that could not have been deduced by any aviation enthusiast who knew something of the principles of vertical take-off and landing. Yet, when the first P.1127 carried out its initial precarious hovers at Dunsfold in 1960, it was generally regarded as yet one more of the V/STOL prototypes which, around this time, were aimed at reconciling the engineering problems of combining the basing flexibility of the helicopter with the combat performance of a jet attack fighter. It was, perhaps, understandable that the P.1127 generated no special excitement in the hearts and minds of the Naval Staffs at the time, nor was there any greater enthusiasm for its battle-field potential among the Air Staffs. It was subsonic; it was not planned to carry a range of sophisticated electronics; it had a pitifully small payload-radius performance compared with contemporary competing projects using conventional take-off and landing; and it did not replace any existing service aircraft which were on the verge of becoming obsolescent.

From 1960 to 1964, many problems were overcome in the development of the P.1127.

Interestingly, the biggest problem did not arise so much from V/STOL itself as from reconciling the engineering conflict between providing acceptable V/STOL qualities and satisfactory transonic flying qualities in a single airframe. The military services continued to show little more than polite interest in the aircraft's puny operational capability, although the P.1127 programme had, by then, considerable government support, mainly on the basis of research contracts.

All this faint and distant interest among Air and Naval Staffs changed positively, however, when the Hawker P.1154 – the first practical supersonic fighter design to feature vectored thrust – won NBMR3 early in 1962. The UK government of the day advised the RAF and RN to take a serious look at this aircraft to meet their future needs ashore and afloat, anticipating that a basic common design could be evolved with the aim of economizing in future defence procurement.

The Royal Navy first received a practical demonstration of V/STOL potential on 8 February 1963, when Bill Bedford – at that time Hawker's chief test pilot – flew the P.1127 prototype, XP831, to a deck landing on the aircraft carrier HMS *Ark Royal* in Lyme Bay, off Portland. Between 8 and 13 April 1963, Bedford and fellow test pilot Hugh Merewether, neither of whom had any carrier experience, took XP831 through the full range of vertical and short take-offs and landings without experiencing any difficulties whatsoever. Contrary to naval preconceptions, the P.1127 met no 'cliff-edge' downdraught effects in hover crossing the catwalks, island turbulence proved no problem and the deck neither buckled nor got red hot.

Unfortunately, the Royal Navy regarded the whole demonstration as something of a non-event. The Fleet Air Arm's Senior Admiral commented that for the first time in his experience of a new jet coming aboard, the 'fright factor increment' was negative. Normally, aircraft undergoing deck trials for the first time were heavier, faster and more heart-stopping than their predecessors. The observers aboard the *Ark Royal* failed to appreciate the importance of XP831's significant reversal of this trend; the most significant misjudgement was betrayed in the subsequent Naval PR handouts which accorded only passing mention to the fact that the aircraft had been flown from the *Ark Royal* by two pilots who had never before landed on or taken off from a carrier.

The deck trials with the P.1127 did little to change the opinions of the Royal Navy. They stuck determinedly to their requirement, in the P.1154, for a two-seat, radar-equipped, supersonic, all-weather fighter to be catapult-launched from the decks of their carriers, *Victorious*, *Eagle*, *Ark Royal* and the projected new 50,000-ton attack carrier CVA-01. The RAF's needs in the P.1154 programme were for a single-seat, attack/strike aircraft with a secondary supersonic intercept capability. However, the Royal Navy's interest in the P.1154 also ultimately foundered. For eighteen months following the completion of P.1154 project studies for the Royal Navy and the RAF at Kingston in 1962, design studies were conducted in an attempt to incorporate the conflicting requirements of the two services into the P.1154 design. The resulting compromise was unacceptable to either. After 1963, the Royal Air Force initiated a separate programme for the design, development and prototype manufacture of a definitive P.1154RAF, but the

Royal Navy went its own way towards the Rolls-Royce Spey-powered McDonnell F-4K Phantom II. With that, the Royal Navy's interest in V/STOL became moribund, and was to remain so while it still possessed the carriers that could accommodate the aircraft it wanted.

The RAF's P.1154 fared no better. The reappraisal of British defence commitments which followed the accession to power of the Labour Government in October 1964 led, in February 1965, to the cancellation of the P.1154 RAF when the first aircraft was about one-third complete. It was some consolation to the RAF that they were permitted immediately to embark on the development of a fully operational version of the subsonic P.1127. Additional F-4 Phantoms were to be acquired for the RAF, and Britain also began a development venture with the aim of acquiring a variable geometry multi-role aircraft, which was eventually to result in the Tornado, after following a long and tortuous route via the F-111 and the Anglo-French VG project. For the Royal Navy, the decisive blow fell in 1966 when the service lost its roles and mission struggle following a further revision of

Test pilot Bill Bedford, flying Hawker P.1127 XP831, makes the first V/STOL landing aboard ship – HMS *Ark Royal*, in Lyme Bay, off Portland – on 8 February 1963.

An early Harrier GR.1 of No. 1 Squadron, based at RAF Wittering, on a low-level flight over the English countryside.

aircraft to be granted a Release for Service Flying, in 1964.

The Kestrel looked similar to the P.1127 but incorporated many different features as a result of experience with the earlier machine. A swept wing of new design was fitted, as was a tailplane with a pronounced anhedral and wider span to improve longitudinal stability, and a longer fuselage, revised air intakes and a repositioned engine were other major changes. The powerplant was the 15,500lb thrust Pegasus 5. Two wing hardpoints, each able to carry a 100 Imp. gallon fuel tank, were installed and a small gunsight was fitted to allow tracking evaluation. The Kestrel could reach Mach 1.25 in a dive.

The Tripartite Kestrel Evaluation Squadron was formed at RAF West Raynham with pilots and ground crew from the RAF, the US Air Force, the US Navy, the US Army and the *Luftwaffe*. During 1965, some 650 flying hours of testing were conducted in England, to evaluate the practical merits of jet V/STOL, developing operational concepts where the aircraft was used in the field and away from conventional air bases. These trials were a considerable success. In 1966, after the evaluation programme, six Kestrels were shipped to the United States, where they were used for US tri-service and individual service trials on land and at sea under the designation XV-6A. These had a particular impression upon the US Marine Corps, who became seriously interested in the XV-6A as a land- and ship-based tactical aircraft. NASA Langley used the XV-6A for flight research through to the early 1970s.

UK defence policy which dictated that tactical air power at sea would, from then on, be provided by land-based aircraft operated by the Royal Air Force. With that came the cancellation of CVA-01, leaving the Royal Navy with a fleet of ageing carriers whose expiry in the 1970s would effectively eliminate Britain's seaborne, fixed-wing combat aircraft capability.

THE KESTREL

Meanwhile, more restrained and immediately practical developments were taking place. In the spring of 1962, the Governments of the United Kingdom, the United States of America and the Federal Republic of Germany negotiated a tripartite agreement to continue the P.1127 development programme and to provide nine aircraft and eighteen engines for a joint evaluation of V/STOL operations in the strike fighter role, using the aircraft in the field, away from conventional air bases. British Ministry of Defence Specification FGA D&P was produced to define the requirements for the Evaluation Squadron aircraft. The sixth P.1127, XP984, was modified considerably during its manufacture in 1963 to become the prototype of the nine Evaluation Squadron aircraft. The new aircraft was given the name Kestrel, after the common European falcon. It was the first jet V/STOL

THE HARRIER

Even as the P.1154 programme was being wound up early in 1965, Kingston was further instructed by the British Government to modify the Kestrel to take a 19,000lb version of the Pegasus, fit the avionic systems then being developed for the P.1154 (less the radar), change the aircraft to accommodate a considerable weapons load and deliver the resulting attack fighter to the RAF in four years' time. The Harrier was the aircraft which resulted from this work. Representing a more than 90 per cent redesign of the Kestrel, it was committed to production in 1967 and entered service with the RAF in 1969. After the formation of the first RAF squadron in April of that year, many changes were subsequently made to the aircraft; notable amongst these was the engine performance, which was raised from the

A Harrier of No. 3 Squad-
ron waits for a No. 20
Squadron aircraft to land
during Exercise 'Grimm
Charade', Germany, 1973.

19,000lb of the Pegasus 101 through the
20,000lb of the 102 to the 21,500lb of the 103
and 104. The weapons system was extended and
augmented by the addition of a passive radar
warning system and, latterly, laser ranging and
marked target seeking equipment. RAF
Harriers are deployed in the ground attack,
reconnaissance and close air support roles,
aiding UK ground forces on the flanks of
NATO (Norway to the Eastern Mediterranean)
and on the NATO Central Front. They spend
over 75 per cent of their time flying at low level
(500 feet or less above the ground) at high speed,
in the region of 400 to 500kts. Survival in any
future hostile situation in the NATO theatre
necessitates low-level missions, and the Harrier
and its weapons system are optimized for use in
this difficult and demanding environment. Most
importantly, however, the aircraft is designed to
operate away from the vulnerable bases which it
uses in peacetime. Low-pressure tyres, self-
contained starting, simple systems check-out
procedures, rapid turn-round between sorties,
low maintenance demands and many other
features which facilitate forward deployment
are all the result of deliberate engineering
choices in the design.

THE TWO-SEAT HARRIER
The two-seat Harrier is a training and two-crew
(operational) version of the single-seat aircraft
stemming from an RAF contract issued in 1966

A two-seat Harrier T.
Mk. 2 trainer on a test
flight from Dunsfold. All
RAF Harriers were later
retrofitted with the
Pegasus Mk. 103 engine
and redesignated T.
Mk. 4.

The two-seat Harrier is cleared to fly from ships but is not used operationally from decks. The version used by the Royal Navy is designated T. Mk. 4N. (Royal Navy)

for a two-seat V/STOL trainer which would be combat-capable. It carries the same weapons and is fitted with the same operational equipment as the single-seaters, and it would be used in battle alongside the single-seat Harriers, flying similar missions from the same forward sites and strips. With two crewmen, it has a basic weight only 1,450lb greater, and this requires less than 250ft of additional STO ground roll to become airborne with the same mission weight of fuel and ordnance as the single-seater. Handling qualities and performance in flight are very similar to the standards of the single-seat Harrier, and spares and maintenance requirements are also much the same.

The Harrier T.2 entered service with the RAF in 1970. In addition to the two-seaters operated by No. 233 OCU at RAF Wittering, each RAF Harrier front-line squadron also operates two-seat aircraft. All RAF two-seat Harriers have been retrofitted with the 21,500lb Pegasus 103 and as such are designated T.4s. The introduction of the two-seat Harrier meant that, after 1970, the RAF was able to convert new pilots, with only 300 to 350 total flying hours, on to the Harrier with safety and economy, the basic V/STOL conversion course involving 22 sorties and less than twelve hours' flying. Today, 50 per cent of the RAF's Harrier squadron pilots are on their first operational tour. The two-seat Harrier is cleared to fly from ships but is not used operationally from flight decks. The version used by the Royal Navy is designated T.4N.

Such, in broad outline, is the story behind the development of the V/STOL concept which, in turn, led to the evolution of the Harrier, its engine and systems. Although the Royal Navy had lost interest in V/STOL with the demise of the supersonic P.1154 project and acquired the conventional F-4 Phantom, when the idea of a seaborne Harrier was resurrected at a later date there were those who said that such an aircraft would simply serve as a stop-gap until something better came along. They were wrong.

The BAe Harrier T. Mk. 4N.

The first real interest in a naval Harrier came not from the Royal Navy but from the US Marine Corps. American interest in the P.1127 V/STOL concept, begun in 1958, had continued throughout the early 1960s, culminating in strong participation by the US Navy and the USAF in the tripartite evaluation programme during 1964–65. Before that, in 1962, the Assistant Secretary to the US Army, Dr. Larsen, had visited Kingston and, during the following months, recommendations were drawn up for a US manufacturer to enter into negotiations with Hawker to develop the P.1127 for use by the US Army. This led, in January 1963, to an agreement between Hawker Siddeley Aviation and the Northrop Corporation under which Hawker were to provide design information and research experience for the further development of the P.1127 in the United States. Later that year, a Northrop team worked alongside the P.1127 designers at Kingston for a time and also carried out a survey of the possible applications of V/STOL in support of the US Army in Germany. The thinking at this time was that a derivative of the P.1127 could probably be used to replace the Grumman OV-1 Mohawk in the battlefield reconnaissance role. However, such a version of the P.1127 was stifled by a rigid interservice delineation of roles and missions which limited the weight of fixed-wing aircraft that could be operated by the Army.

Although the development of the US Army P.1127 – and therefore the collaboration between Northrop and Hawker Siddeley – thus came to an end, six of the nine Kestrels which had been used by the Tripartite Evaluation Squadron at West Raynham were shipped to the United States in 1966 for further evaluation by the US Air Force, US Navy and US Marine Corps, although the last had not taken part in the trials at West Raynham. The trials that followed included deck operations from the 60,000-ton attack carrier USS *Independence* and the 13,900-ton assault ship USS *Raleigh* and continued for more than three years, but while the US Navy and Air Force regarded the whole operation primarily as a research programme,

AV-8A Harrier 58393 of VMA-231 'Ace of Spades', USMC.

A USMC AV-8A at the hover.

the USMC gradually became convinced that V/STOL was the key to some of its more pressing operational problems.

USMC REQUIREMENTS

To the USMC, the infantryman is the most important person in the organization. Everything is designed to provide him with all the services and back up that he needs to succeed in his fighting task. He is always at the sharp end. The US Marine Corps prides itself on its reputation gained during combat over some two hundred years, and the lessons learned in past conflicts have proven the concept of a lightly armed, mobile, hard-hitting force.

It is because it is lightly armed – lacking its own massed heavy artillery and tank formations – that the USMC relies so heavily on fire support from the air, and it was because of the deficiencies experienced in this field, particularly during the Korean War, that the USMC first investigated the use of V/STOL in the battle-

field support role. Initially, this resulted in the development of the helicopter gunship which was to be used to such good effect in Vietnam.

Trials with the XV-6A had shown that the aircraft in that form lacked the power and combat capability to fulfil the Marine Corps requirement. However, the advent of the RAF's Harrier GR.1 changed the picture completely: here, at last, was the capability of combining effective and survivable close support with the basing flexibility of the helicopter. In September 1968 two US Marine Corps pilots, Col. Tom Miller and Lt. Col. Bud Baker, test-flew the Harrier GR.1 at Dunsfold and subsequently made a highly favourable report on the aircraft's capabilites to their Chief of Staff, Gen. McCutcheon, in Washington. Following further evaluation by a US Navy test team in 1969, the USMC ordered a total of 102 single-seat and eight two-seat Harriers under the respective designations AV-8A and TAV-8A in a six-year procurement programme.

Two of the chief reasons why the USMC gave up its planned acquisition of two squadrons of F-4 Phantoms in 1969 in order to initiate procurement of this 'foreign' V/STOL aircraft were the Harrier's ability to operate from small, rapidly prepared sites close to the battle zone, thus reducing the time taken to respond to a call for air support from the infantry to the trenches; and its ability to fly from helicopter assault ships such as the LPD (aft platform) and LPH (through-deck) types and so provide beach-head air cover in the absence of large attack carriers. From the start of the US Navy Board of Inspection and Survey Trials early in 1971, therefore, the AV-8A Harrier was committed to become the first of the breed to operate regularly from ships at sea. Only one structural modification was incorporated to fit the aircraft for deck flying – tie-down lugs on the outrigger oleo legs.

There were many disbelievers and sceptics in the Corps, in the US Navy and in Congress. Here was a foreign attack fighter, designed to British rules for a land-based air arm, which the USMC were proposing to operate from ships which had neither catapults nor arrester wires!

The incredulity is perhaps best summed up in the words of a startled Member of Congress who, in one of the various Committees which in 1969 seemed endlessly to debate the USMC's wish to procure the first twelve Harriers straight off the Kingston production line, contributed the immortal comment: 'Colonel! Ya mean to tell me this Limey airplane can operate from the fantail of a cruiser!?'

Perhaps the key figure during this period of USMC V/STOL history was Admiral Elmo R. Zumwalt USN, the Chief of Naval Operations. Zumwalt was convinced that the Navy was not devoting sufficient ship procurement resources to quantity, as distinct from quality or capability. He contended that his service was neglecting the sea control mission, for which much larger numbers of less capable combat aircraft-carrying ships would be necessary. He therefore set in motion studies aimed at defining a simple carrier which could be procured in the ratio of seven or eight such ships for the cost of one large attack carrier (CVA), and the Sea Control Ship evolved as a simple 15,000-tonne displacement, garage type 'flat-top',

propelled by a single screw to a maximum speed of only around 20kts, without catapults or arrester wires but capable of operating an air group of twenty aircraft, a mix of V/STOL attack fighters and anti-submarine warfare (ASW) helicopters. It was the first concept for a purpose-built Harrier-carrying ship.

CONCEPT EVALUATION

The first AV-8As underwent their first US Navy Board of Inspection and Survey Trials at Patuxent River in February 1971. These included deck-landing trials on the USS *Guadalcanal* and *Coronado*, as a result of which the aircraft was cleared to operate from this type of vessel. The following month Marine Attack Squadron 513 (VMA-513) was formed with ten AV-8As under the command of Col. Baker.

Having taken delivery of the AV-8As, the USMC began to tailor the Harrier's capabilities to fit its tactical requirements, refining and developing the art of close air support. As a result of operating experience two major changes were recommended for the Marine Corps aircraft. The first was the removal of the Ferranti 541 inertial nav/attack system, which had proved too complex in operation for the USMC's purposes and had an adverse effect on reaction time. The second was the replacement

of the Martin-Baker Type 9 Mk. 1 ejection seat with an American design, the Stencel S3S-III, which was lighter than its British equivalent and featured a faster parachute deployment. Further deliveries of AV-8As enabled two more Marine Corps attack squadrons, VMA-231 and -542, to equip with the type. Although an agreement had been signed between Hawker Siddeley and McDonnell Douglas for the licence manufacture of the Harrier in the United States, all AV-8As and TAV-8As procured by the USMC were in fact built in Britain, with McDonnell Douglas responsible for various engineering tasks and modifications.

In 1973, while VMA-231 and -542 got used to their aircraft, VMA-513 found itself participating in the bureaucratic battle to prove the concept of the purpose-built Harrier-carrying vessel, the Sea Control Ship. To provide data for the study, the aircraft flew from the deck of the USS *Guam*, which was operating as an interim Sea Control Ship, in North Atlantic waters and in weather conditions too severe to permit the ship's helicopters to fly. In 1974–75 this unit and ship completed a six-month detachment with six AV-8As to the US Sixth Fleet in the Mediterranean, as a result of which the concept of a Sea Control Ship/AV-8 weapon system proved to be both practical and powerful.

TAV-8A two-seaters of VMAT-203, the USMC's Harrier conversion unit.

The question of how V/STOL aircraft would be integrated with flight deck operations in a large fleet carrier was also unequivocally answered when a detachment from VMA-231 went aboard the carrier *Franklin D. Roosevelt* (CV-42) of the Sixth Fleet, operating in the Mediterranean in 1976–77. The ship was packed with aircraft, for, in addition to the fourteen USMC Harriers, she carried her conventional Air Wing's full complement of F-4 Phantoms and A-7 Corsairs. The experiment lasted ten months. The USMC Harrier pilots totally convinced an initially sceptical Air Group that their V/STOL attack fighters could operate outside the constraints of the traditional deck cycle, without the ship turning into wind for launch or recovery, and could perform effective air defence and attack tasks alongside Phantoms and Corsairs. During the experiment, all conceivable options were tried aboard the carrier, and at no time did the Harrier fail: on the contrary, it was proved beyond all doubt that the factors limiting ship operation at sea resulted from the deployment of conventional catapult-launched aircraft.

Meanwhile, after Admiral Zumwalt had completed his term as CNO and retired in 1974, the US Navy had quietly dropped the idea of the Sea Control Ship. However, the US Navy acknowledged that it did have a future requirement for its own supersonic jet fighter, termed the V/STOL Type B. No significant budgets were provided for the pursuit of this goal,

except for the XFV-12A Thrust Augmented Wing project, which, after many years of research and development and with over $80 million spent, was abandoned by 1980.

During the early years of AV-8A operations, six aircraft were kept permanently at the US Air Base at Kadena in Okinawa, Japan, the three front-line AV-8A squadrons taking turns to man this detachment and supply, typically, eight pilots. Usually, the pilots sent to Kadena had already been flying together for some time, and the result was a highly integrated, experienced team of flyers supported by ground and maintenance crews dedicated to provide a high level of operational serviceability. The Kadena detachment produced a number of important results and vindicated the USMC land-based concept.

On average, each of the pilots in the AV-8A detachment at Kadena flew about 27 hours in a four-week period, but of more significance was the tendency for the number of sorties flown and their duration to be consistent. The maintenance cycles per aircraft were therefore high in comparison to other types on the USMC inventory, which in general made longer though less frequent sorties.

The training programme at Kadena covered the full range of V/STOL operations with the exception of carrier recoveries. Missions usually comprised low-level tactical training over land and sea, together with extensive medium-level air-to-air combat training, including VIFF

Vectoring in forward flight (VIFF): pitch change.

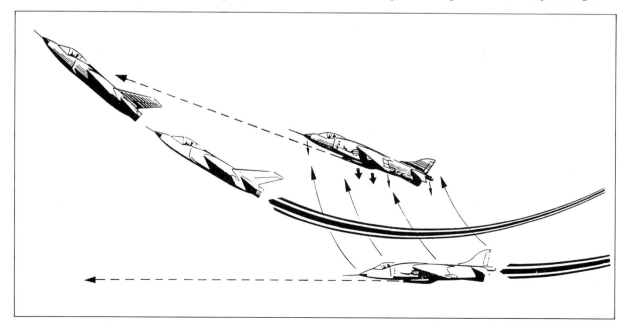

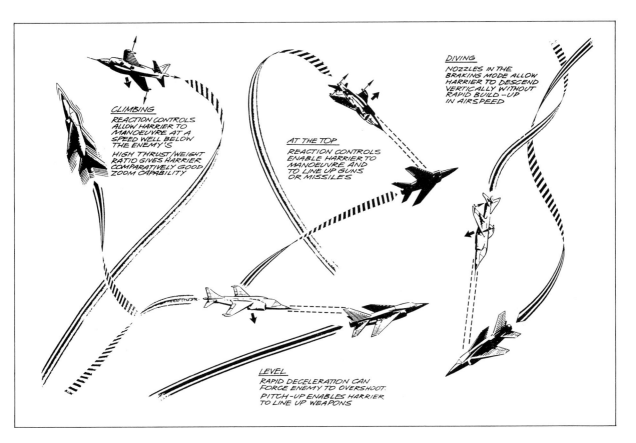

CLIMBING
REACTION CONTROLS
ALLOW HARRIER TO
MANOEUVRE AT A
SPEED WELL BELOW
THE ENEMY'S

HIGH THRUST/WEIGHT
RATIO GIVES HARRIER
COMPARATIVELY GOOD
ZOOM CAPABILITY

AT THE TOP
REACTION CONTROLS
ENABLE HARRIER TO
MANOEUVRE AND
TO LINE UP GUNS
OR MISSILES

DIVING
NOZZLES IN THE
BRAKING MODE ALLOW
HARRIER TO DESCEND
VERTICALLY WITHOUT
RAPID BUILD-UP
IN AIRSPEED

LEVEL
RAPID DECELERATION CAN
FORCE ENEMY TO OVERSHOOT.
PITCH-UP ENABLES HARRIER
TO LINE UP WEAPONS

Advantages of VIFF.

(thrust vectoring in forward flight). A Harrier/ AV-8 pilot can deflect the engine thrust when in combat simply by operating the nozzle lever, giving an additional manoeuvring capability, with large attitude changes and rapid speed variations; the aircraft can still be controlled at extremely low speeds using its reaction control system. VIFF is extremely useful in situations where the pilot needs to achieve a high angle of attack or reduce his radius of turn in order to bring his sights to bear on an opponent. When members of VMA-542 were posted to Kadena and exercised VIFF during air combat manoeuvring training, to a man their view was that the AV-8A was the only aircraft in that theatre of operations capable of engaging an F-15 and overcoming this USAF fighter's advantages in manoeuvrability.

However, the majority of sorties in Japan were tactical air support missions, integrated with such ground elements as the 3rd Division of the USMC, which was deployed there at the time. During one deployment from Kadena an interesting experiment was organized on the island of Ishima, some 18 miles to the north of Okinawa. This involved V/STOL operations

from a semi-prepared surface of crushed, compacted coral. Support for the AV-8As during this exercise was provided by a C-130 Hercules which also operated from the strip. Special refuelling and re-arming techniques were used, utilizing standard C-130s as ground tankers. This enabled the turn-round time to be reduced to a minimum.

The USMC found that the tactical significance of the operations at Ishima were considerable because a crushed coral strip can be prepared more quickly and at less cost than one made from most other materials. Despite the very high ambient temperature prevalent in Okinawa, especially during the July–August period, there were no operational limitations on the aircraft in their V/STOL modes. Water injection was used at all times and water system performance checked as a matter of course at every take-off. The six Harriers based in Japan were the first USMC AV-8As to be equipped with the on-board oxygen generating system (OBOGS), which concentrates the gas from the engine bleed air, eliminating the need for liquid or gaseous oxygen replenishment.

Although the trials flown by Bill Bedford and Hugh Merewether with the P.1127 prototype on HMS *Ark Royal* in February 1963 were so disappointingly and inappropriately received by the Royal Navy, and despite the fact that the P.1154RN programme had failed so abysmally in 1965, the practicality of naval V/STOL was emphasized by further evaluation which took place during the next few years.

From 18 to 20 June 1966, Bill Bedford flew Kestrel XP894 from the commando carrier HMS *Bulwark* in a series of trials designed to gain experience in the mixed operation of V/STOL aircraft and helicopters in amphibious assault operations. Similar trials were carried out in 1969 by an early production Harrier GR.1, XV758, which flew from *Bulwark* with wing drop tanks and rocket pods, and in August of that year another GR.1 operated from the helicopter platform of the 12,100-ton cruiser *Blake*, successfully operating in conditions that included a wind-over-deck (WOD) of up to 35kts and a ship roll of ±6°.

In March 1970 two RAF Harrier GR.1s deployed aboard the 50,000-ton fleet carrier HMS *Eagle*, as a result of which the aircraft was cleared for deck operations by RAF pilots. Between 4 and 15 May 1971, the pilots of No. 1 Squadron – the first RAF unit to equip with the Harrier in 1969 – carried out a full squadron deployment on board *Ark Royal* in the Moray Firth. The Harriers had previously been prac-

tising on their own runway at RAF Wittering, part of which had been painted to simulate a carrier deck. Some publicity was given at the time to the notion that this was the first occasion since the Second World War that an operational RAF squadron had flown off an aircraft carrier. In fact it was not: No. 209 had done it with its Pioneers in the early 1960s, during the Indonesian confrontation.

It must be emphasized that the purpose of these trials was to evaluate further the Harrier under operational conditions, and to assess the feasability of deploying the RAF's V/STOL force aboard aircraft carriers to assist in amphibious warfare operations. Nevertheless, the success of the seaborne Harrier deployments undoubtedly influenced the Royal Navy's active contemplation of restoring its case for the continuation of fixed-wing aviation at sea after the retirement of *Ark Royal*, its last 'traditional' aircraft carrier.

THE 'THROUGH DECK CRUISER'

In the late 1960s, the Royal Navy had been forced to re-appraise its maritime air task. In the wake of the cancellation of the projected 50,000-ton carrier CVA-01, it became British defence policy that, when the life of existing Royal Navy carriers expired in the 1970s, tactical air power at sea would be provided by land-based aircraft operated by the Royal Air Force. Although similar ideas had proved to be completely unworkable in the past – in the Far East at the end of 1941, for example – the thinking was that Royal Navy surface forces in their NATO role could, in theory, rely on an air 'umbrella' provided from NATO shore bases. There was, of course, no inkling that the Royal Navy would one day have to fight a war some 8,000 miles from the nearest RAF land base.

The Navy's position in terms of V/STOL carrier operations was summarized soon after the publication of the 1966 Defence White Paper, by J. W. Powell DSC RN (Ret), who had recently given up the post of Assistant Director Naval Warfare:

'Why not V/STOL planes operating from platforms on ships, without catapult or arrester gear? The arguments are unchanged and largely immutable: for VTOL you need a power-to-weight ratio of 1.2 – for conventional purposes successful aircraft are flying with ratios as low as 0.35, and at 0.75 to 0.9 the most spectacular performance is obtained. In the future, no one will deny that the VTOL trick, with better engines, will be enhanced, but it will never surpass the horizontal variety. The question is, will the cost-effectiveness of a ship-plus-V/STOL aircraft system be worthwhile? Probably the answer will be in the affirmative but one must not be hasty: the essential overheads in the ship, parking space, workshops, magazines, etc. all remain unchanged and they will surely make it totally cost-ineffective to operate less than sixteen to twenty-four aircraft – about 15,000 to 20,000 tons in fact.

'At this point we must look quickly at the philosophy of the ship – should she operate purely as parent to her one squadron of aircraft? At this sort of size, surely it is worth putting in command facilities, warning radar and ASW helicopters? There are perfectly good reasons, too, why it might be sensible to combine the role with that of a Commando-ship replacement; or, greatly to increase the range of the aircraft, we can give them a longer deck for STO, or maybe a little catapult . . .'

The kind of vessel advocated by Commander Powell would in fact come to fruition, albeit in a rather roundabout fashion. So would his 'little catapult', in the ingenious disguise of the ski-jump. Reflections such as these, by influential senior officers, persuaded the Royal Navy not to accept as totally inevitable the loss of its organic fixed-wing air power.

In the late 1960s the Naval Staff began studies of a new class of ship, much smaller than the cancelled CVA-01 and without catapults or wires, which was intended for operations with a rotary-wing air group in NATO waters. The fact that she had a through deck and was therefore theoretically capable of operating V/STOL aircraft was played down. The design was committed to manufacture in 1972 as HMS *Invincible* (CAH-01), the first of a new class of ASW carriers.

During her design and building periods, at a time when the term 'aircraft carrier' had been politically discredited, *Invincible* was variously described as a 'through deck cruiser', 'command cruiser' and 'anti-submarine cruiser'. Nevertheless, she was and still is an aircraft carrier, regardless of her other roles, and the more succinct titles were gradually dropped with the growing realization, stemming from major exercises, that naval surface forces could not be satisfactorily protected solely by shore-based air power, even in NATO waters.

The eight Sea Harriers of No. 809 Naval Air Squadron lined up at RNAS Yeovilton in 1982 prior to their departure to Ascension Island and the South Atlantic.

NAVAL HARRIER DEVELOPMENT

From 1971, studies were requested from Hawker Siddeley (Kingston) to define the minimum changes that would be necessary to turn the Harrier GR.3, then in production for the Royal Air Force, into an aircraft which would meet the fighter, strike and reconnaissance role which the Directorate of Naval Air Warfare in MoD (Navy) had set out in a Naval Staff Target. The budgets allocated to these studies were exceedingly tight, and the survival of what was seen as a high-risk programme was crucially dependent on the strict adherence to narrow constraints in terms of both engineering and economics.

The naval Harrier's AI radar, essential for the air interception and fighter roles against long-range maritime patrol and shipborne attack aircraft, was to be derived from the Ferranti ARI 5979 Sea Spray radar, then being developed for the Lynx helicopter. Sea Spray, which in its helicopter-borne configuration was to be used in conjunction with the Sea Skua anti-ship missile, was designed to detect and track small targets such as missile-armed fast patrol boats. Wide- or narrow-angle sector scan was used in the search mode, while monopulse tracking was employed in azimuth once the target had been located. The head-up display (HUD) was to be developed from the existing Smiths Industries equipment fitted in the RAF's Harrier GR.3s. An inertial navigation system (INS) was considered for a time and then rejected because of its high cost and the problems of aligning it at sea.

Much preliminary design work had already been completed by November 1972, when Hawker Siddeley received a contract to proceed with further study. Project and feasibility studies were completed and assessed, and the avionics systems gradually became more realistic as operational capability was analysed. Design work throughout proceeded under the direction of Dr. John W. Fozard, Chief Designer (Harrier).

In 1973, a second phase of competitive tenders against a revised navigation and attack system was initiated, encouraging the use of all-digital avionics. The Royal Navy were now becoming more confident in defining their real needs for the aircraft, and had identified a somewhat healthier budget than the Kingston team had earlier anticipated. No increase was demanded in mission performance over that which the Harrier GR.3 could be expected to

provide after allowing for weight changes in the Royal Navy version, and no thrust increase was specified for the naval version of the Pegasus engine, the GR.104.

Apart from the avionics, the changes from the Harrier GR.3 (as eventually defined) were a new front fuselage with a raised cockpit to provide more panel space and console width as well as better visibility; a new cockpit and conditioning system; provision for twin generators on the engine; a revised hydraulic system; a completely redesigned electrical system; increased roll RCV power; increased tailplane travel; a revised liquid oxygen system; a simple autopilot; and an independent emergency brake system. Modifications to the stores pylons, provision for air-to-air and air-to-surface missiles, and the fitting of a Martin-Baker Type 10 zero-zero rocket ejection seat completed the changes.

With design studies completed, Kingston prepared and submitted a formal Development Cost Plan, a necessary preliminary to programme initiation. By the closing months of 1973 agreement had been reached in Whitehall that the naval Harrier programme was to go ahead, and even the name that was to be bestowed upon the new aircraft had been narrowed down to two choices: it would be called either Osprey or Sea Harrier.

Then followed a series of political and economic crises which threw the whole programme into disarray. In 1973, on the very day on which it had been planned to announce the launching of the Sea Harrier programme in the House of Commons, Parliament instead found itself debating the world's first fuel crisis. This was followed, in rapid succession, by the British mineworkers' strike and the economic catastrophe that resulted in the three-day working week, all followed by a change of government in 1974.

At Kingston the Harrier team soldiered on, barely sustained by a trickle of small study fundings, and it came as something of a surprise to industry when, in May 1975, Roy Mason – then Secretary of State for Defence – announced that his Government had approved the development and production of an initial batch of twenty-four Sea Harrier FRS.1 aircraft for the Royal Navy on a fixed-price contract. The aircraft were to operate from the new aircraft carriers *Invincible* and *Illustrious*, and also from the conventional, 23,900-ton, light fleet carrier *Hermes*. The plan was for each vessel to have a peacetime air group of five Sea Harriers and ten

A diagram showing the changes incorporated in the basic Harrier GR.3 airframe to produce the Sea Harrier.

A Sea Harrier FRS.1, carrying 190-gallon ferry tanks and AIM-9 Sidewinder missiles, demonstrates the ski-jump technique. As the camouflage indicates, this photograph was taken after the Falklands War.

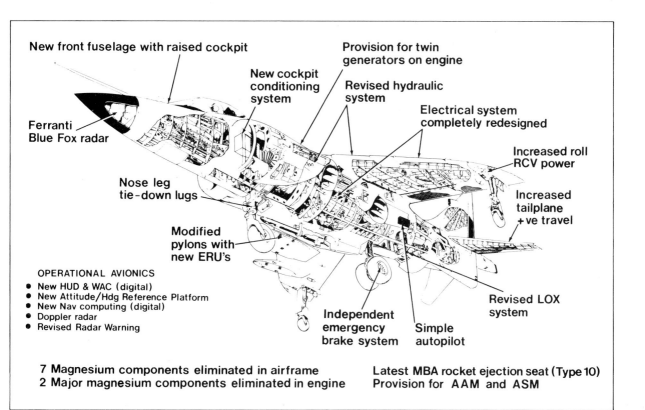

New front fuselage with raised cockpit

Provision for twin generators on engine

New cockpit conditioning system

Revised hydraulic system

Electrical system completely redesigned

Ferranti Blue Fox radar

Increased roll RCV power

Nose leg tie-down lugs

Increased tailplane +ve travel

Modified pylons with new ERU's

OPERATIONAL AVIONICS
- New HUD & WAC (digital)
- New Attitude/Hdg Reference Platform
- New Nav computing (digital)
- Doppler radar
- Revised Radar Warning

Revised LOX system

Independent emergency brake system

Simple autopilot

7 Magnesium components eliminated in airframe
2 Major magnesium components eliminated in engine

Latest MBA rocket ejection seat (Type 10)
Provision for AAM and ASM

Sea King ASW helicopters, the remaining Sea Harriers equipping a shore-based Headquarters and Training Squadron.

THE SKI-JUMP

Meanwhile, technological developments were in hand to enhance the Sea Harrier's take-off performance. In the early 1970s, a Royal Navy officer, Lt. Cdr. Taylor, had drawn attention to the potential of launching a Harrier-type V/STOL aircraft from an upward-inclined ramp. His thesis was written at Southampton University in 1973, and the Harrier team at Kingston-upon-Thames, which had become involved with Taylor's work a year earlier, subsequently continued studies of the so-called 'ski-jump' principle using knowledge and computer aids outside the scope of Taylor's academic exercise. Considerable company funding was invested in these studies which, during 1974 and early 1975, confirmed that the performance gains promised by the ski-jump launch were very important.

Study funding was obtained from the UK Ministry of Defence in 1975, and advanced investigations were started. Simulator work showed particularly encouraging results in respect of flying qualities and handling, and late in 1976 Hawker Siddeley Aviation received a contract to design and build a practical ski-jump ramp. The test ramp was designed for a range of angles from 6° to 20° and consisted of 40 steel channels, each 2ft 6in wide and 40ft long, mounted on an adjustable support structure. It was fabricated and erected by British Steel (Redpath Dorman Long, at Scunthorpe) in the space of five months and was ready for use on a runway at the Royal Aircraft Establishment, Bedford, by July 1977. The first Harrier tests were carried out on 5 August 1977, using XV281, a GR.1 trials aircraft, and by 7 September, when the first phase was completed, 73 launches had been conducted; a further 43 launches were made by a Harrier two-seater, the launch speeds varying between 53 and 113kts. All were made with the ramp set at 6°.

In September 1977, as a result of this testing, the Royal Navy decided that a similar ramp should be fitted to *Invincible*, which had been launched by HM The Queen in May of that year, and by mid-1978 this ship had been fitted with a 7° ramp at the forward end of her flight deck. The height of the ramp was limited to avoid interfering with the firing arc of the warship's Sea Dart missile launcher, which restricted the choice of ski-jump exit angle. Meantime, the angle on the trials ramp at RAE Bedford had been increased to 9° in October 1977; this was stepped up to 12° in January 1978, and 15° in April. Owing to the un-availability of test aircraft, trials with a ramp exit angle of 17½° were not completed until the end of 1978, while final tests with the ramp angle at its maximum 20° began in April 1979.

This broadside shot of HMS *Hermes* ploughing through the Atlantic shows the ski-ramp to good advantage.

During 1978, while these trials were in progress, the Royal Navy had reached the decision that *Hermes*, then a helicopter-only ASW vessel and due to embark the first Sea Harrier squadron in 1980, was to be fitted with a 12° ski-jump during a scheduled refit in 1979, while the second Royal Navy command cruiser, *Illustrious* – launched into the River Tyne by HRH Princess Margaret on 30 November 1978 – was fitted with a 7° ramp, the same configuration as that carried by her sister ship, *Invincible*. The third ship of the class, *Ark Royal*, laid down in December 1978, was to be fitted with a 12° ramp, following the re-positioning of her Sea Dart launcher.

In simple terms, the advantage of the ski-jump is that it enables the aircraft to leave the deck at a speed much lower than is needed in a flat-deck take-off at the same gross weight. The initial upward trajectory from the ramp curves over towards the horizontal and this allows the aircraft some ten seconds in which to accelerate to a speed at which the upward forces equal the aircraft's weight. From this point in the launch the pilot completes a normal transition to wingborne flight by slowly rotating the nozzles of the engine fully aft. Significant take-off performance gains are achieved using the ski-jump, allowing a 60 per cent reduction in deck length for given launch conditions, or an increase of over 30 per cent in military load capacity compared with the same flat-deck run. Alternatively, these benefits can be traded for a lower WOD, demanding lower speed, and consequently a lower fuel consumption, from the ship. Launches are not significantly affected by crosswinds, and aircraft handling during a ski-jump launch is easier than during a flat-deck launch. The effect of ship pitching motion on STO launches from flat-deck ships can be severe, but with the ski-jump technique the pitch motion allowance can be much reduced since the aircraft's initial trajectory is *always* away from the sea. The upward initial flight

A fine photograph of a Sea Harrier launching from the ramp of HMS *Hermes* in a plume of spray.

Sea Harriers on the
production line at British
Aerospace's Kingston
factory.

30

path also increases the safety margin for the pilot in the event of a handling error or malfunction at launch.

SEA HARRIER PRODUCTION

An initial production batch of 24 aircraft, plus three development aircraft (DB), were ordered to expedite testing and clearance, and while the first Sea Harrier neared completion in the summer of 1978 the testing of its entire range of operational equipment was under way in two specially modified Hawker Hunter T.8 two-seaters, XL580 and XL602. The first of these flew on 9 January 1978 and went to British Aerospace at Dunsfold; the other went to the Royal Signals and Radar Establishment (RSRE) at Bedford. A third Hunter T.8M, XL603, was later added to the contract as a reserve aircraft. On completion of their development trials, the Hunters were to be handed over to the Royal Navy as airborne weapon system trainers.

At 5.45pm on 20 August 1978, chief test pilot John Farley took the first Sea Harrier FRS.1, XZ450, for its maiden flight from Dunsfold. Still in its yellow primer, XZ450 was not a prototype: it was in fact the first aircraft of a production order that had now risen from 24 to 31. On this initial flight Farley made three vertical take-offs, one short take-off, several conventional landings, performance hovers and a deceleration, transition and vertical landing, logging a total flying time of 35 minutes. He described the flight as 'uneventful' and was enthusiastic about the improved visibility provided by the raised cockpit. The Sea Harrier's modified air brake presented no difficulties during the flight. XZ450 appeared at the SBAC display, Farnborough, in September and was retained for trials at Dunsfold. On 13 November it became the first Sea Harrier to land on an aircraft carrier, HMS *Hermes*.

In addition to the production batch, three development Sea Harriers had been ordered in 1975. The first of these, XZ438, was flown by M. H. B. Snelling on 30 December 1978 and was subsequently retained by the manufacturers at Dunsfold for performance and handling trials. The second, XZ439, flew on 30 March 1979 and went to the A&AEE Boscombe Down for stores clearance trials, while the third, XZ440, flew on 6 June 1979 and was employed in handling and performance trials at Dunsfold and Boscombe Down and with the RAE and Rolls-Royce (Bristol).

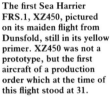

The first Sea Harrier FRS.1, XZ450, pictured on its maiden flight from Dunsfold, still in its yellow primer. XZ450 was not a prototype, but the first aircraft of a production order which at the time of this flight stood at 31.

Because of its very high thrust-to-weight ratio, the Harrier enjoys many of the characteristics of a supersonic fighter, for example a rapid climb and a high acceleration; in addition, it can make use of its unique VIFF feature. This agility is obtained for a very modest fuel usage, the Pegasus turbofan requiring a full throttle fuel flow of the order 250lb/min (110kg/min), compared with at least three times this rate for a reheated conventional fighter of equivalent performance.

Like most subsonic fighters, the Harrier can cruise at altitude at more than Mach 0.8 for well over an hour on internal fuel; at low level, cruise speeds between 350 and 450kts are achievable for fuel flow rates of about 75lb/min (35kg/min), depending on configuration, and the aircraft can accelerate rapidly to 600kts. Internal fuel capacity is 5,060lb (2,277kg), and external combat fuel can total 1,600lb (730kg). The normal external capacity load is 5,000lb (2,270kg) in addition to the two 30mm guns.

Armed with 30mm guns and Sidewinder AAMs, the Harrier can respond rapidly in an off-the-deck alert (less than two minutes from alarm to airborne in VTO without the ship changing either course or speed). The intercept radius at high altitude is up to 400nm, allowing three minutes for full throttle combat and fuel reserves for VL on return to the ship. The aircraft can carry out both electronic and visual surveillance from either low or high altitude: in one hour, flying at low level, it can survey some 20,000 square miles of sea. All of a wide range of standard UK/USN/NATO stores and ordnance – rockets, free-fall bombs, retarded bombs, flares, etc. – as well as anti-shipping weaponry can be carried and delivered in a range of attack manoeuvres.

However, the chief role of the Harrier is close air support, and the Sea Harrier has retained all the features of the earlier versions which contribute to intensive operations from austere land bases – low pressure tyres, self-containment for starting and servicing etc; the aircraft can thus perform the same functions as the AV-8 in support of amphibious assault either from a

ship's deck or from within a beach-head. Even so, a Harrier cannot usefully decelerate to a hover, dunk and listen – helicopters do this better – and the Sea Harrier cannot at present interrogate sea sensors, but its rapid VTO-off-the-deck reaction to a call to lay a sonobuoy screen, or to carry air-drop torpedoes to a contact point, is unique. The total time from alarm to a drop point 30 miles distant is under six minutes.

It was the Sea Harrier's capability to carry out this wide variety of missions and roles, with an equally wide assortment of weaponry, which dictated the evolution of its systems and their operation. Some of them are unique, as, indeed, is the aircraft itself.

COCKPIT SYSTEMS

Access to the cockpit is gained by a portable ladder which clips into the footsteps and handholds on the starboard side of the front fuselage. The cockpit is larger compared with those of earlier versions of the Harrier, in order to maximize operational efficiency. Panel space and console width have been increased, and the entire layout of instruments and controls has been revised to ease the pilot's workload. The latest available miniature equipment (for example, warning caption modules) has been used, and white night lighting is provided, mostly by edge-lit panels.

Flight, navigation, attack and weapon-aiming information is presented to the pilot as a head-up display (HUD) in the pilot's display unit (PDU). Essential HUD data is written over the radar display to facilitate monitoring, and conventional dial instruments provide a complementary head-down display (HDD) of flight information. A centralized warning system (CWS) provides the pilot with an audio and/or visual indication of aircraft system failures and other cautionary information. The visual warnings comprise primary (red) or secondary (amber) captioned window lights, primary warnings being accompanied by an audible tone in the pilot's headset from the communication system.

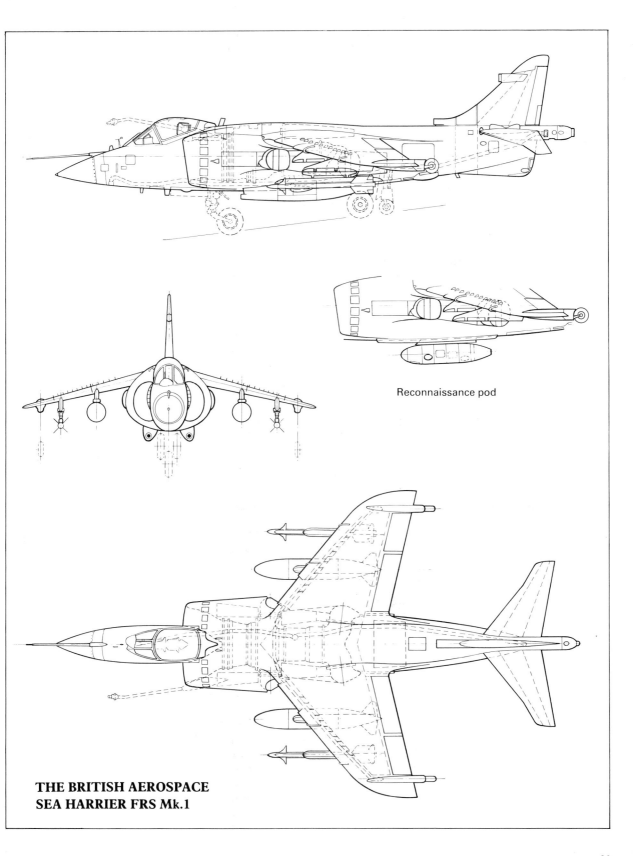

Reconnaissance pod

**THE BRITISH AEROSPACE
SEA HARRIER FRS Mk.1**

Raising the pilot's seat eleven inches compared with that of the Harrier GR.3 has improved his view in all directions, particularly aft, and provides more space for equipment below the cockpit floor. Since all the structure of the front fuselage is new, better access for servicing has been incorporated in the assemblies, not only in the pressurized zone but also below the floor and ahead of the windscreen.

Oxygen is supplied to the pilot on demand from a five-litre liquid oxygen (LOX) unit which is mounted in the rear equipment bay on a tray and fitted with self-sealing, quick-disconnect, push-in couplings. An alternative gaseous oxygen (GOX) system can be fitted. The contents are displayed to the pilot on a cockpit gauge. Either 100 per cent oxygen or 'airmix' can be selected: for the latter, the ratio of air to oxygen is reduced as altitude increases, reaching 100 per cent oxygen at 30,000ft cabin altitude. An emergency supply of gaseous oxygen is mounted on the ejection seat and provides ten minutes' endurance. This supply can be disconnected by the pilot if the normal system fails, and is switched on automatically on ejection.

Cabin conditioning air is supplied from the sixth stage of the engine's high-pressure compressor. Some of the air is cooled by passing it through a cold air unit. It is then mixed with uncooled air in proportions governed by a temperature control valve, and passes through a water extractor before being discharged into the cockpit. To maintain cooling on the ground and in V/STOL flight, the depression in the engine inlet is used to force air through the heat exchanger. Cabin discharge air is used to cool the radar. In the event of condensation occurring on the transparencies, hot air direct from the engine compressor can be selected for rapid demisting. Emergency ventilation is provided through a ram air intake on the aircraft nose.

The Sea Harrier is equipped with a Martin-Baker Type 10 rocket-propelled ejection seat which allows safe ejection down to zero forward speed at zero altitude. An explosive miniature detonating cord (MDC) shatters the canopy as part of the automatic ejection sequence (ejection is initiated with the canopy closed) and, on ejecting, the harness is automatically tightened and the pilot's legs are restrained. The MDC can be fired on the ground to allow the pilot to escape in the event of a jammed canopy. For external rescue, the MDC is operable from outside the aircraft, from points on either side of the canopy frame. When the seat is operated the IFF and UHF radio are switched automatically to transmit on emergency frequencies, and if the aircraft is submerged a sonar beacon in the tail cone is switched on automatically to assist in its location.

HYDRAULIC SYSTEMS

Two independent hydraulic systems operating nominally at 3,000psi provide power for the aileron and tailplane flying controls. Each system is supplied by an engine-driven pump and pressure is maintained by accumulators. In addition to providing power for the flying controls, No. 1 system powers the undercarriage, air brake, flaps, q-feel units, fuel flow proportioner, wheel brakes, nosewheel steering and windscreen wiper. In the event of pressure loss in No. 1 system, No. 2 system maintains power to the flying controls. The undercarriage can be lowered and the air brake raised by pressurized nitrogen stored in bottles, while accumulators provide emergency power to nosewheel steering and the wheel brakes. If No. 2 system fails, or the engine fails, a ram air turbine (RAT) extends into the airstream automatically and provides emergency power to the flying controls.

ELECTRICAL SYSTEMS

A 12kVA alternator, connected from the engine through a constant-speed drive, provides 200V, 400Hz, three-phase electrical power. The main 28V DC busbar is supplied from a 5kW transformer-rectifier unit. In normal operation this busbar is connected to the essential and non-essential services busbars, both of which are disconnected from the main busbar should the main generator fail. The non-essential services busbar loads are then not supplied, and the essential DC busbar loads are met by the aircraft's 24V, 18 amphour batteries. Two sources of power are available when the engine is not running: a ground power unit which can be connected externally, and the aircraft's internal APU (auxiliary power unit) which drives a 6kVA alternator. The APU can also provide emergency electrical power in flight.

FUEL SYSTEMS

Fuel is contained in seven integral tanks – five in the fuselage and two in the wings – providing a usable volume of 632 Imp. gallons, and 100

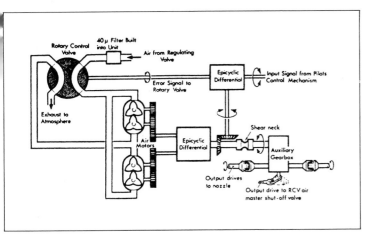

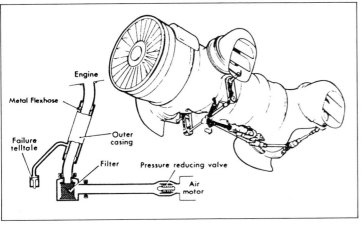

Location and operation of the nozzle actuators.

nozzle fairing. A probe can be fitted to the port intake cowling, permitting refuelling in flight. The probe is illuminated for night refuelling.

In addition to normal drop tank jettisoning, wing tank fuel can be dumped in three and a half minutes from either or both wing tanks. If external tanks are retained their contents are jettisoned through the wing tanks.

Demineralized water (50 Imp. gallons) is carried in a fuselage tank between the rear engine nozzles. Injected to restore engine thrust in hot ambient conditions, it is delivered by a turbopump driven by engine bleed air.

ENGINE CONTROL SYSTEMS

The Pegasus is a simple, robust and reliable, two-shaft, vectored thrust turbofan. The pilot can vary the length and direction of the thrust vector by rotating the nozzles to specific angles, from fully aft through 100° to about 20° forward of vertical. Three key systems operate the Pegasus engine: the nozzle actuation system, which controls the nozzles; the throttle box, which controls speed; and the reaction control system, which provides the supplementary aerodynamic control systems in V/STOL flight.

Logically, the nozzle actuation system should be part of the engine, but as a result of historical accident in the early P.1127 days, it became (and still remains) an aircraft-provided system, using HP air to generate mechanical power in an air motor. This is distributed to the four nozzles by a system of shafts, bevel gears and chains. As the system is an unduplicated flying control (apart from the dual-wall air supply flexhose and the twin-rotor motor), it must therefore fail 'safe', in that the nozzles should remain synchronized whatever else happens. The NAS system is simple, reliable and fast in operation. Nozzle rotation at over 90°/sec is achievable, and it is satisfactorily precise as a servo-system, an angular positional accuracy of the order of ±1° being attained at the nozzles.

Excluding the engine nozzles, their bearings and the final nozzle drive chains (engine-supplied items), the NAS weighs 120lb, representing less than 1 per cent of the aircraft's empty operating weight and a satisfactory price to pay for a device which vectors accurately the 30,000 jet horsepower output of the Pegasus engine. System power is sufficient to vector the nozzles with the external airloads appropriate to over 450kts air speed.

The use of a nozzle lever alongside the throttle lever in the cockpit is perhaps the

Imp. gallon combat tanks or 330 Imp. gallon ferry tanks can be carried on the inboard wing pylons. The system is designed for operation with Avtag (JP4), Avtur (JP8) or Avcat (JP5) fuels. To minimize its vulnerability to combat damage and to maintain the aircraft within its CG range, the system is divided into two approximately equal parts, either of which can supply the full engine demand. Fuel is pumped to the engine through a hydraulically operated flow proportioner supplied by electrically driven booster pumps mounted in negative-*g* compartments.

Fuel is transferred from the port drop tank, to the port wing tank, into the two front tanks, and then to the port centre tank. The starboard drop tank and wing tank feed the rear tank and thence the starboard centre tank. Compressor bleed air from the engine at 6psi assists in the delivery of the fuel of the centre tanks and prevents it from boiling at altitude. The aircraft is pressure-refuelled on the ground through a single coupling housed inside the port rear

greatest single simplifying idea in the vectored thrust concept. This configuration has been used since the very first transitions of the P.1127 in 1961. The operation of the nozzle lever is in the same sense as the throttle: both act as 'push-forward-to-go-faster' controls. The VTO stop locates the lever (and hence the nozzles) at the correct setting for VTOL, that is, with jets truly vertical at the wheels-on-ground attitude of the aircraft. If the lever is lifted, further aft movement becomes available and gives up to 20° of nozzle angle for reverse thrust.

The STO stop can be pre-set before take-off. It allows the pilot to select the scheduled angle (in the range of 40° to 60°, depending on weight) by feel alone when the correct unstick speed or the deck end is reached after 5 or 6 exhilarating seconds of almost 1g acceleration in the ground or deck roll. All V/STOL modes can be safely flown by pilots using only the left hand. Procedures use constant nozzle angle with varying throttle or constant throttle with varying nozzles, but a new device allows the nozzles to be nudged ±10° from their VTOL setting without use of the nozzle lever (when the wheels are down and the air brake inoperative) by thumbing the speedbrake switch located on the top of the throttle lever. Hence 'nudging' provides about ±0.2g acceleration/deceleration at fixed aircraft altitude for as long as the switch is held over, thus giving a 'speed trim' facility in hovering flight. In some high-workload situations it is desirable for the pilot to keep his hand on the throttle at all times, and in the hover the throttle acts as the height control. Throttle lever gearing is designed to give about 0.1g per inch of travel, and a local handrest is provided to facilitate the precise control needed in vertical flight where throttle lever movements of as little as 8mm are needed.

The Harrier is controlled in normal wing-borne flight by conventional ailerons, rudder and all-moving tailplane. The ailerons and tailplane are power-operated by tandem hydraulic jacks fed by two completely independent hydraulic systems, and the rudder is operated by the pilot. A limited-authority monoplex autostabilizer operates in the pitch-and-roll and yaw channels at speeds up to 250kts; it is provided to reduce pilot workload and is not essential for safe, accurate control in the V/STOL modes.

In hover, and in partially jetborne flight below the normal aerodynamic stalling speed, the conventional controls naturally have

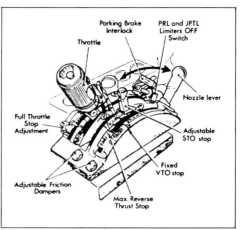

Harrier cockpit throttle box.

insufficient effectiveness, and they are therefore augmented by air jets from the reaction control system. This system makes use of engine HP compressor bleed air which is ducted to shutter valves located at all the extremities of the aircraft. These reaction control valves (RCV) are simple convergent nozzles each closed by a swinging shutter, driven by a linkage from the local flying control, which varies the exit area. Thus the rear (nose-down) pitch valve shutter is driven by a linkage from the tailplane, the yaw RCV by a linkage from the rudder and the wing-tip (roll) RCV by a linkage from the adjacent aileron. Having no local flying control, the front (nose-up) pitch RCV is driven by a linkage directly off the pilot's control column.

The design standards for the reaction control system are stringent and the environmental conditions harsh. It operates as an unduplicated primary flying control in V/STOL and must meet appropriate safety and reliability criteria. The system was satisfactorily demonstrated in rig testing and in flight and qualified to these

Harrier reaction control system.

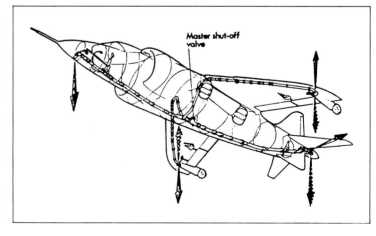

standards. It weighs a little over 200lb and at maximum control demand in hover is transmitting and directing total energy (in the form of hot compressed air) at a rate of about 3,000hp over distances of about 20ft. Bleed air flows through the RCS ducts automatically when the engine nozzles are rotated downwards from fully aft. There are no complicated pilot checks or selection procedures. A single small pressure gauge in the cockpit, reading pressure in the duct branch to the front RCV, informs the pilot that the system is live when the nozzles have been selected down.

VECTORED THRUST OPERATION

Vectored thrust V/STOL offers unique advantages over conventional flying and other forms of V/STOL, but is it necessary to deal with the two persistent myths. VTO is not extravagant of fuel. The Pegasus is a turbofan engine, and running at its maximum rating in VTO, it does not result in uneconomic consumption. Full throttle fuel flow is only some 220lb per minute: no other comparable jet fighter can get into the air from a runway or a ship using as little as 100lb of fuel (under 30 seconds at 220lb/min), and a similar aircraft in afterburner will use at least three times this amount to become fully airborne. It is, however, true that the Harrier cannot lift its maximum payload from VTO. Nevertheless, it can lift about half its normal maximum STO load of fuel plus ordnance in VTO, and no other aircraft can lift half its maximum disposable load from its minimum take-off run.

Flexibility of operation in VTO is a key factor in the Harrier's combat use, ashore or afloat. Wind direction is not important, the VTO spot need be no bigger than that required by a large helicopter and little fuel is used in taxying. A lightweight aluminium mat about 70ft square is adequate for VTOL operation from natural sites on land. On board ship, the Harrier can lift off from its parking spot, the vessel need not turn into the wind, and response time is minimized: the Harrier can start up and and be airborne within two minutes if the pilot is already strapped in. No special deck protection is required, and no hazard to flight deck crew and equipment is offered outside a 30ft radius.

As for all fixed-wing aircraft, an airstream blown over the wing of the Harrier provides lift, and it is, therefore, no surprise to find that the Harrier can lift greater loads in STO, at speeds of 50kts and upwards, than in VTO. Even at the highest mission loads, launch speeds are very much lower than those of a conventional jet fighter, because only about one-third of the gross weight (at most) is carried by aerodynamic lift. The ground or deck roll distance to achieve these STO speeds is very modest because of the high acceleration with nozzles aft. Maximum loads can be lifted from a 1,200ft ground roll, or from about half this distance on a flat-decked ship (depending upon windspeed). Time taken to unstick (nozzles down to about 50°) is, typically, 5 to 7 seconds.

The nosewheel steering system is very precise, giving accurate and easy tracking in STO, enabling narrow runways (40ft wide on deck) to be used although about 50 per cent greater width is used ashore where crosswinds are more frequently encountered. Site preparation for a STO strip is minimal. Little more fuel is used in STO than in VTO, the Pegasus delivering the same thrust from the same fuel flow. Acceleration is marginally lower at the high gross weight flow in an STO launch, so the fuel 'penalty' is, say, 5 more seconds to weight-on-wings flight at less than 4lb per second.

On returning from a mission with its fuel load reduced, the Harrier can hover even if its armament is unexpended. Recovery is, therefore, by vertical landing. Unlike VTO, full throttle is not required in VL, so hover fuel flow is reduced to about 180lb per minute. The transition from 200kts of wingborne speed to the hover takes less than 30 seconds and typically requires 0.5 nautical miles in still air. The fuel used to hover is well under 100lb, as high thrust is needed only as airspeed falls away towards zero. In the hover, a Harrier can reposition itself over distances of the order of 1,000ft in less than half a minute. Approach and transition are not to a precision touchdown but to a hover near the intended VL spot. Pilot workload is therefore much reduced, safety is increased, and worse weather can be tolerated than is the case with a conventional jet, while overshoots or 'go-rounds' are almost entirely absent in VL recoveries. As a result of these factors, fuel reserves can be much smaller.

WEAPONS AND NAVIGATION SYSTEMS

The Sea Harrier weapons system is divided into three components, the Ferranti Blue Fox radar, the Smiths Industries head-up display and weapon aiming computer (HUD/WAC) systems and the Ferranti navigation, heading and attitude reference system (NavHARS). Blue Fox is an I-band, pulse-modulated radar designed for the dual roles of airborne interception and air-to-surface search and strike. The scanner, electronic control amplifier, transmitter-receiver, signal processor and nine line replaceable units (LRUs) are mounted together in the nose, accessible inside the folding nose cone. The radar interfaces primarily with HUD/WAC, providing target range and bearing, scanner azimuth and elevation angles and angle-rates for use in the target interception and weapon aiming equations. It operates in the following modes:

1. Search, in air-to-air and air-to surface roles.
2. Detection, against air and surface targets.
3. Lock-on track. The automatic tracking provides range and angle inputs to the HUD/WAC for gun and air-to-air missile attacks. For discreet targets, range and angle information is used in ballistic equations in the HUD/WAC.
4. Lock-on jam, the tracking of jamming targets.
5. Radar lock-on, to visual targets.
6. Air-to-surface ranging, along the radar bore-

sight, which is slaved to the aiming mark in the HUD.
7. Navigation. An alternative to B-scan, a ground stabilized mapping PPI display can be selected to update the navigation systems. The radar antenna is stabilized by the navigation system and sweeps in wide angle azimuth search through ±30° in pitch. The pilot can select from two pulse widths, 1- or 2-bar scan, and a frequency agility mode which reduces clutter and the effects of jamming.

The second element of the weapons system, the head-up display and weapon aiming computer system, contains a powerful, fully programmable computer which interfaces with most of the avionic equipment fitted on the aircraft. It provides the following functions:
1. Display of aircraft attitude and heading.
2. Display of other flight information by pilot selection: indicated air speed (IAS) or Mach number, barometric or radar altitude, angle of attack, sideforce and vertical speed.
3. Display of navigation aids (navaids): tactical air navigation (tacan), UHF homing and micro-

In 1983, HMS *Invincible* and No. 801 Squadron went to Australia for a series of major exercises. Ship, aircraft and crew received an enormous welcome from the population, the Sea Harriers attracting large crowds at air displays in Sydney and Freemantle. During the exercises the Harriers emerged clear victors in air combat against Mirage IIIs of the Royal Australian Air Force.

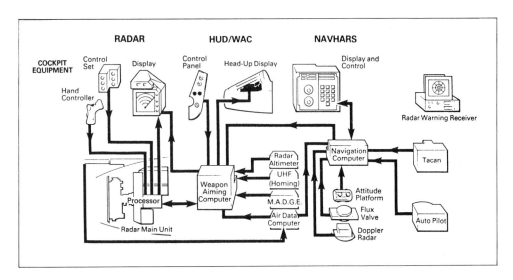

Sea Harrier avionics layout.

An unusual view of an AV-8A of the Spanish Navy aboard the aircraft carrier *Dédalo*, photographed through the head-up display of another Harrier.

wave aircraft digital guidance equipment (MADGE).

4. Computation and display of all air-to-surface weapon aiming in manual and automatic release modes with a continuously computed impact point (CCIP) solution or a manual, depressed sight line (DSL) mode.

5. Solution of air-to-air aiming equations.

6. Display of air-to-air symbols.

7. An integral, independent standby sight.

The primary modes displayed in the HUD on selection by the pilot are V/STOL, launch, general, air-to-air, air-to-surface, reversionary weapon aiming and bearing for use during

NavHARS alignment. The system incorporates a built-in test facility and the software can easily be adapted for different weapon characteristics and combat tactics.

The third element is the navigation, heading and attitude reference system, which, together with a Decca 72 doppler radar and a Sperry flux valve, forms the navigation system. The system takes two minutes to align, either at sea or ashore, and the system can be readily updated with an 'on top' tacan or radar fix. The NavHARS consists of three LRUs, one of which is in an all-attitude, twin-gyro, three-accelero-meter platform measuring the aircraft's attitude and acceleration. The second LRU is a computer which controls the platform erection and all the navigation computation functions, and the third is a combined display and control unit in the cockpit for the pilot. The system can display the following information:

1. Present position in latitude and longitude or tactical grid reference.
2. Range, bearing, course-to-steer and time-to-

go to ten waypoints, all of which can be assigned a velocity.
3. Estimates of time remaining on task derived from fuel gauge and flow-meter computer inputs.
4. Range and bearing to tacan station or offset.
5. Wing speed and direction.
6. Ground speed and track.

In addition, a number of ancillary units and sensors play a part in the integral weapon system operation, including tacan with an offset facility, UHF homing and MADGE. Other avionics, separate from the integrated nav/attack system, are U/VHF radio, standby UHF radio, radar warning receiver (RWR), IFF/SIF, an I-band transponder and a voice recorder.

ARMAMENT

The Sea Harrier FRS.1 has seven weapon stations. The wing and centreline stations are equipped with standard twin-piston ejector release units (ERUs) for the carriage and release of a variety of stores. The port and starboard

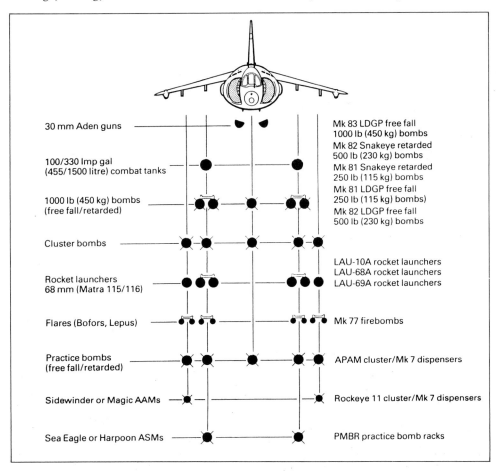

30 mm Aden guns	Mk 83 LDGP free fall 1000 lb (450 kg) bombs
	Mk 82 Snakeye retarded 500 lb (230 kg) bombs
100/330 Imp gal (455/1500 litre) combat tanks	Mk 81 Snakeye retarded 250 lb (115 kg) bombs
	Mk 81 LDGP free fall 250 lb (115 kg) bombs)
1000 lb (450 kg) bombs (free fall/retarded)	Mk 82 LDGP free fall 500 lb (230 kg) bombs
Cluster bombs	
	LAU-10A rocket launchers
	LAU-68A rocket launchers
Rocket launchers 68 mm (Matra 115/116)	LAU-69A rocket launchers
Flares (Bofors, Lepus)	Mk 77 firebombs
Practice bombs (free fall/retarded)	APAM cluster/Mk 7 dispensers
Sidewinder or Magic AAMs	Rockeye 11 cluster/Mk 7 dispensers
Sea Eagle or Harpoon ASMs	PMBR practice bomb racks

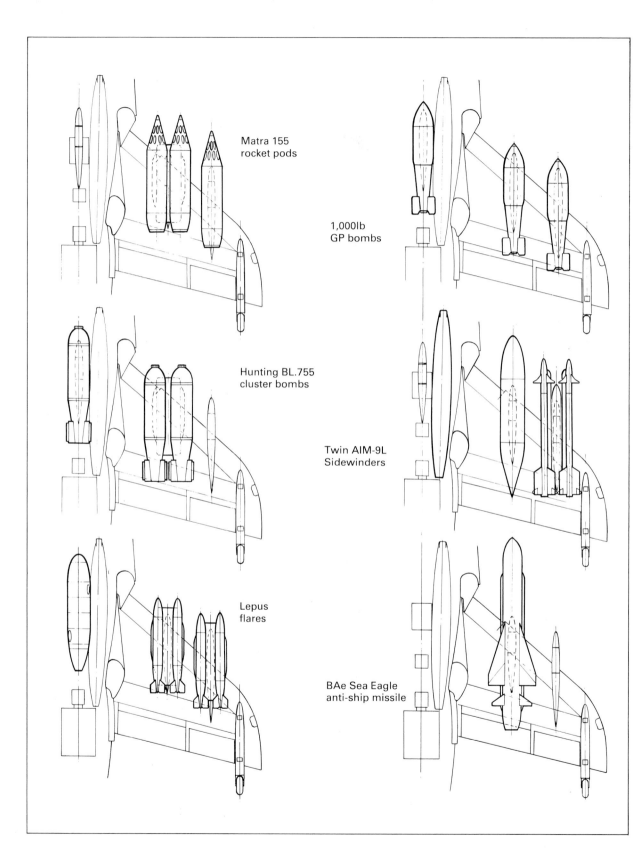

Matra 155
rocket pods

1,000lb
GP bombs

Hunting BL.755
cluster bombs

Twin AIM-9L
Sidewinders

Lepus
flares

BAe Sea Eagle
anti-ship missile

Development Sea Harrier
showing twin AIM-9L
Sidewinder installation.

fuselage stations are exclusively for the carriage of 30mm Aden guns in pods.

The inboard wing stations and the centreline station each have maximum capacities of 2,000lb, and each outboard station has a maximum capacity of 1,000lb. The inboard stations can carry jettisonable fuel tanks of either 330 or 100 Imp. gallon capacity. The outboard wing pylons can be fitted with either single or twin LAU-7A/5 AIM-9 launch rails, and the seventh station, on the centreline, can carry a reconnaissance pod.

As the accompanying line drawings illustrate, the Sea Harrier has been cleared for the carriage and release of a wide variety of British, US and NATO armament, including free fall, retarded and practice bombs, cluster bomb units, rockets, flares and air-to-air missiles. The aircraft operates with the AIM-9L Sidewinder air-to-air infra-red homing missile, and can also carry the British Aerospace Sea Eagle long-range anti-ship missile. Missiles such as Harpoon, Martel, and Magic are also compatible.

Close-up view of the twin
AIM-9L installation.

5 SPANISH MATADORS

The Spanish Navy provides an excellent illustration of how the Harrier concept can offer considerable capability at much less cost and complexity than can a conventional fixed-wing naval aircraft, and with much greater flexibility. In October 1972, John Farley, then Hawker Siddeley Aviation's Chief V/STOL Test Pilot, flew a Harrier from Dunsfold direct to the Spanish Navy's helicopter carrier *Dédalo*, at sea off Barcelona, and landed vertically on the vessel's wooden flight deck. For the next two days, Farley conducted flight operations which convinced the Spanish Navy that Harrier jet V/STOL was the way their future should be directed.

SPANISH NAVAL AIR CAPABILITY

The advantages of flexible air cover and extended support to the Spanish Navy in operating tactical aircraft were clear. The Harrier was a cost-effective and appropriate solution for a navy with limited means, but its acquisition by the Spanish was not a straightforward process. In the first place, helicopters were the only aircraft flown at sea by the Spanish Navy (which had no experience of operating fixed-wing aircraft since the Spanish Civil War), although the Harrier's V/STOL characteristics would at least be within the understanding of its pilots. Second, aircraft carriers are expensive to build and operate, and the Navy did not have the funds to so do. *Dédalo* was the only Spanish carrier, she was on a five-year lease from the US Navy which was due to expire in 1972 and, more seriously, she was an old ship which meant that she was not capable of operating contemporary conventional tactical aircraft. The Harrier's characteristics would offer a cost-effective and appropriate solution to parts of these problems.

Not the least of the problems was that it required an Act of Parliament to enable the Navy to own and operate tactical aircraft at all, and even then the Act restricted them to shipboard use. Moreover, the Navy's decision to acquire Harriers was further complicated by the political sensitivity of relations between Spain and the United Kingdom. At that time, 1973–74, General Franco was in power, and the UK did not view the right-wing dictator's Government with favour. Just before the Harrier demonstration had been arranged, the British Labour Government had cancelled a Spanish order for frigates placed at a British shipbuilding yard, and the demonstration Harrier was refused permission to overfly Spain en route to *Dédalo*. The Spanish Government and senior Spanish Navy officials did not consider that a defence equipment deal with the

A line-up of AV-8As and TAV-8As of *Escuadrilla 008* at Rota.

44

An AV-8A of *Escuadrilla 008* at the hover, Rota.

United Kingdom would proceed smoothly, if at all, and the contract was therefore channelled through the United States with the co-operation of the US Government and the US Navy.

PROCUREMENT AND TRAINING

Six single-seat and two two-seat Harriers were ordered from Kingston by the UK Government on behalf of the US Government, as part of the Fiscal Year 1974 US Marine Corps procurement. In 1976 these aircraft, designated AV-8A and TAV-8A, respectively, were shipped to the United States carrying US Bureau of Aeronautics (BuAer) numbers. Never having operated tactical jet aircraft, the Spanish Navy had to set up an entirely new training and command system. Ten pilots – all familiar with helicopters and a few having a modicum of light aircraft experience – were sent to the USA to undergo conversion and training in fixed-wing jet operation up to TA-4 Skyhawk standard.

The Spanish pilots went to Whitman Air Force Base to be converted by a joint UK/US industry/service team on to their own Harriers (now renamed Matadors), which were identical to the USMC's AV-8As and TAV-8As apart from radio changes. Their USMC markings were scrubbed off to reveal Spanish roundels and markings underneath. The Spanish pilots' chief instructor at Whitman AFB was a recently retired Royal Air Force Officer, Sqn. Ldr. Ken Jones. Following instrument and cockpit orientation procedures, flying conversion started with taxying, before going to conventional take-offs, and then into vertical take-offs and landings, and short take-offs.

During this transition period, one of the original batch of AV-8As crashed and was destroyed.

The unit into which the Harriers were absorbed was *Escuadrilla de Aeronaves 008*. By the time the six-month Harrier transition programme had been completed, the Spanish Navy's ground crews and engineers had also finished their training, and by late 1976 the *Escuadrilla* had begun to take on its own character. With the arrival of *Dédalo* on the US East Coast, the squadron remained in the USA for a further month for carrier qualification before returning to its main base at Rota at the end of 1976. Accompanying the unit were two US Navy pilots, who stayed until the *Escuadrilla* had completed its combat capability training and was ready to enter service with the Spanish Navy. *Escuadrilla 008* became fully operational in March 1977.

In 1978, an order for five more Matadors was placed with British Aerospace and, since political and economic relations had improved following the death of General Franco and the democratization of the Spanish nation, these aircraft were delivered in 1980–81 direct from the Harrier production line at Kingston under the designations Harrier Mks. 55 and 58 (equivalent to the AV-8 and TAV-8 respectively). A second group of Spanish pilots, not all of them with helicopter qualifications, had followed the first to the USA, where they were trained, first on the T-34 Mentor and then on fixed-wing jets with the US Navy, before transferring to No. 233 Operational Conversion Unit at RAF Wittering in the United Kingdom for their V/STOL conversion. Subsequent groups

of pilots undertook their fixed-wing jet training with the US Navy and their carrier conversion at Rota using *Escuadrilla 008*'s TAV-8s.

IN SERVICE

Since acquiring its Matadors, *Escuadrilla 008* has achieved a high standard of efficiency. Under its normal flying training programme, the Matadors are deployed to a number of Spanish Air Force bases such as Valencia and Malaga in addition to operations aboard *Dédalo*. During shipboard deployments the aircraft carry out combat air patrols, anti-shipping strikes and intercept missions against Spanish Air Force aircraft, including F-5s and Mirages.

At Rota, the monthly flying programme is based on a 21-day cycle. The normal flying programme at Rota usually consists of formation work, air-to-air combat training, instrument flying and low-level training, the last typically at 420kts and 100–200ft. Training includes practice operations against units of the Spanish fleet and intercept missions against other aircraft. Normal sorties are of about one hour's duration and each pilot averages two missions per day. In air-to-air combat exercises, it is left to the discretion of the individual pilot as to when and how to use the VIFF capability of the Matadors. These is no limitation, and it can be used in any way, whether to slow down and allow an interceptor to overshoot or to go into a climbing tight turn and outmanoeuvre an attacking aircraft. Once a year, *Escuadrilla 008* deploys to Valencia for a 20- to 30-day period in which weapon training forms the major proportion of the work; this includes bombing using Mk. 76 25lb practice bombs and 5in Zuni rockets and ground strafing with the 30mm

AV-8A No. 9 of *Escuadrilla 008* makes a fast run over Rota for the benefit of the camera.

A TAV-8A Harrier of *Escuadrilla 008*.

Aden guns. Matadors also carry Sidewinders for the air-to-air intercept role.

During seaborne operations over recent years, five or six Matadors with seven or eight pilots have been considered the optimum operating force on board *Dédalo*, but the aircraft carrier has taken up to nine in the past, in addition to four SH3 and four Bell 212 helicopters. A force of five or six Matadors has enabled a group of four aircraft to be lined up on deck for launch in a two-abreast formation, one behind the other. At sea, *Escuadrilla 008* has developed the technique of launching the foremost aircraft down the port side of the ship in a short take-off directly along *Dédalo*'s deck, parallel to the centreline, followed by the foremost starboard-side Matador launching at an angle, steering for the port bow. These two

are followed by the rearmost port-side and rearmost starboard-side aircraft launching along corresponding, criss-cross paths. Using this technique, *Escuadrilla 008* can launch four Matadors in just two minutes. The recovery of returning Matadors is always from the aft port-side station and completed in pairs, usually taking about a minute per pair, followed by a short pause of about one minute whilst the first two taxi to starboard, making room for the next pair.

At sea, *Escuadrilla 008* regularly co-ordinates its operations with a variety of ship types from the Spanish Navy and has the opportunity to fly sorties with or against the US Sixth Fleet in simulated warfare. During these exercises, Matadors engage in mock combat with AV-8As and F-14 Tomcats. In Exercise 'Ocean Venture'

AV-8A Harriers of *Escuadrilla 008* recovering to the carrier *Dédalo*. The Spanish Navy uses its AV-8s to carry out CAP missions, although they are, strictly speaking, strike aircraft.

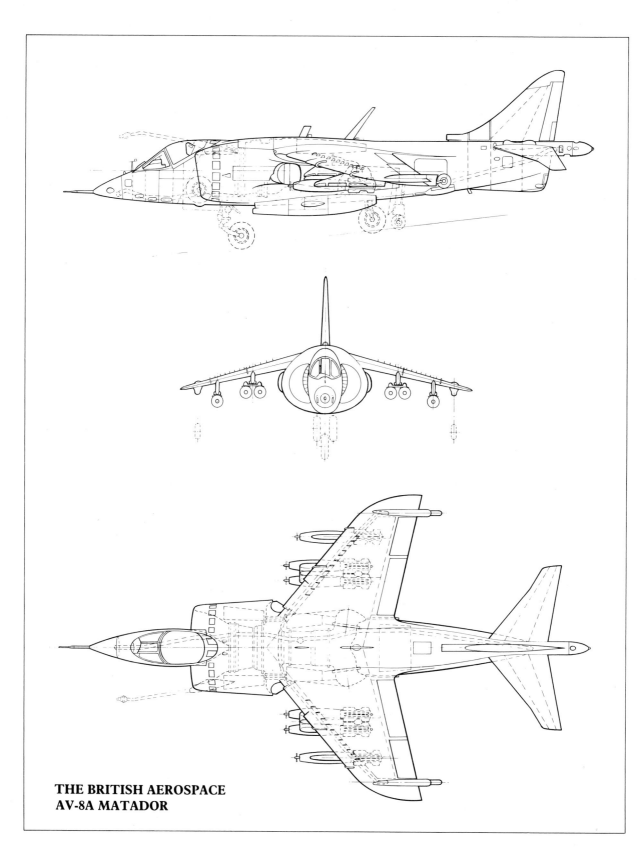

**THE BRITISH AEROSPACE
AV-8A MATADOR**

during 1981, for example, Matadors operated with their USMC AV-8A counterparts from the US amphibious assault support ships *Guam* and *Saipan*. With the former, *Escuadrilla 008* carried out cross-deck operations – the first time such operations had been attempted by a combined US/Spanish force. It proved highly successful. In the joint exercises, Matadors acted as aggressors using the attack group principle, 'attacking' major US naval units as well as playing the role of interceptors in the 'defence' of their own forces.

THE AV-8B/SEA CONTROL SHIP CONCEPT

In 1983, the Spanish Navy became the first export customer for the AV-8B Harrier II, with an order for twelve aircraft, to be established in service alongside the existing Matadors in 1987. The first three aircraft, designated EAV-8B, were delivered in October 1987 to the newly formed *Escuadrilla 009*, which is working up at the time of writing. The Harrier II has brought a new dimension to the Spanish Navy's striking power and will operate from the sea control ship *Príncipe de Asturias*, the first fighting ship to be designed from the keel up as a 'Harrier carrier'.

Like many new warships (the Royal Navy's *Invincible* Class included), she has been over ten years from conception to commissioning.

In the mid-1970s, the Spanish Navy bought the design of the US Navy's projected Sea Control Ship with the intention of being a second-source constructor. However, cancellation of the US Navy's interest in the concept in 1974 caused a delay in the laying down of a Spanish vessel since no US prototype would exist. However, with the direct help of Gibbs & Cox, the well-known naval consultants in New York who had played a major role in the original Sea Control Ship studies for the US Navy in 1972–74, the design of the ship was completed and construction commenced in the El Ferrol yard of Empresa Bazan Nacional about 1977.

Major changes were introduced to the design as a result of the Spanish Navy's own needs and their V/STOL experience and because of recent developments at Kingston in V/STOL operating techniques. Chief amongst the latter was the embodiment of a 12° ski-jump (launch ramp) at the bow. The ramp is to the same basic shape as that fitted retrospectively to HMS *Hermes* in 1980–81, but Gibbs & Cox succeeded in integrating the ramp into the bow flare of the

An AV-8A Matador shortly after touchdown on board *Dédalo*.

ship's hull in an elegant and seaworthy manner, since the changes were effected before the issue of drawings. Launched by HM Queen Sofia in May 1982, *Príncipe de Asturias* provides a handsome and effective sea platform for the Spanish Navy's Matadors and EAV-8Bs until well into the twenty-first century.

Although vertical take-off has brought a new and flexible dimension to Spain's defences, particularly within the context of its NATO commitments, the role of Spain's Matadors and EAV-8Bs remains essentially a seaborne one, their operations including air combat manoeuvres, surface attack, reconnaissance and interception. Tactical air power on land remains the prerogative of the Spanish Air Force. In time of war, the Spanish Harriers would have the task of defending the western approaches to the Straits of Gibraltar, in conjunction with other NATO aircraft, and would, if necessary, be deployed into the Mediterranean to act in concert with the US Sixth Fleet, the Royal Navy and other NATO task forces.

The second production Sea Harrier, XZ451, flew on 25 May 1979 and became the first example to be taken on charge by the Royal Navy, being ceremonially accepted by the First Sea Lord, Admiral Sir Terence Lewin, on 18 June 1979, for service with the Intensive Flying Trials Unit.

INTENSIVE FLYING TRIALS

No. 800A Naval Air Squadron was commissioned at Royal Naval Air Station Yeovilton, Somerset, on 26 June 1979 as the Sea Harrier Intensive Flying Trials Unit (IFTU) and operated initially with XZ451 and one RAF Harrier

T.4, XW927, which was detached from RAF Wittering to RNAS Yeovilton in July. A second Sea Harrier, XZ452, was delivered to the squadron in October 1979, and XZ451 and XZ452 together carried out the Unit's first sea detachment aboard the *Hermes*. XZ455 was delivered in November 1979, to be followed by XZ453, XZ456 and XZ457 in January 1980.

On 31 March 1980, No. 700A Squadron was disbanded and immediately re-formed as No. 899 Headquarters and Training Squadron. Its primary task was to be the Royal Navy's Sea Harrier operational conversion unit (OCU), with a role similar to that of the Harrier OCU at

On 18 June 1979, XZ451, the second production aircraft, became the first Sea Harrier to be taken on charge by the Royal Navy. It was ceremonially accepted by the First Sea Lord, Admiral Sir Terence Lewin.

XZ450 at the hover. On 4 May 1982 this aircraft became the first Sea Harrier to be lost through enemy action in the Falklands War when it was shot down by ground fire over Goose Green. Its pilot, Nick Taylor, of No. 800 Squadron, was killed.

Development Sea Harriers undergoing early trials with Sea Eagle anti-ship missiles. One of these development aircraft was XZ450, which still carried attachments and cockpit instrumentation associated with the Sea Eagle when it was shot down over Goose Green. Argentine intelligence officers who examined the wreckage apparently reached the conclusion that all Sea Harriers with the Task Force were fitted with Sea Eagle, a missile superior to the Exocet, and this may be one of the reasons why large Argentine Navy surface units, with the exception of the *General Belgrano*, did not attempt to engage the Task Force.

RAF Wittering but with Royal Navy opera-
tional training as its main teaching task – not V/
STOL flying training, which was carried out at
Wittering for Royal Navy and RAF crew alike.
A few weeks later, on 11 July 1980, HMS
Invincible was commissioned, and the Royal
Navy's new airborne striking force began to take
shape.

One of the key men responsible for many
aspects of the Sea Harrier's development and
introduction to service was Cdr. Nigel 'Sharkey'
Ward, a very experienced Fleet Air Arm pilot.
Ward joined the Royal Navy in 1962 and, after
gaining his watch-keeping ticket as a seaman
officer in a frigate and minesweepers, began
flying training for the Fleet Air Arm in 1966.
Between 1969 and 1976, he completed two 2½-
year operational tours flying Phantoms with No.
892 Squadron aboard HMS *Ark Royal*,
following which he joined the Directorate of
Naval Air Warfare at the Ministry of Defence in
London, where he first became acquainted with
the Sea Harrier. Early in 1979 he was appointed
Commanding Officer of the first Sea Harrier
squadron, No. 700A, the IFTU.

Cdr. Ward has this to say about the early
training experiences with the Sea Harrier:

'You might logically suppose that the
Intensive Flying Trials Unit would have been
give a precise and detailed programme of trials
to carry out. Not a bit of it! I was told three
things. First, the eyes of the world are on you.
Secondly, get it right (don't let it go wrong)!
And finally (this was extremely helpful), the
Royal Navy's F-4 Phantom IFTU produced
enough paper reports to cover the runway area
that the aircraft needed for landing!

'The latter point was of course a real "let-off"
for my team. Sea Harrier could land vertically
and therefore if I interpreted my instructions
carefully we would not need to produce a tenth
as much paper as our predecessors! (It didn't
work out like that.)

'True as the story is, it provided the first
lesson in V/STOL: conventional runways are
not necessary for this breed of aircraft.

'Creating the ground rules for trials was not
difficult. They can be summarized, principally,
as:

1. Get to know the aircraft backwards.

2. Learn how to fly it to the boundaries of its
operational envelope.

3. Don't crash it.

4. Later would come the evaluation of the
weapon system and new avionics, as well as the
definition of tactics in the three roles of fighter,
recce and strike/attack.

'We borrowed a great deal of V/STOL
handling expertise from the Royal Air Force and
stuck rigidly to their V/STOL standards and
practices. This was to produce for us the best
flight safety record for any aircraft entering
service in the Western World. We also
"borrowed" considerable upper air handling
experience but had to combine this with the
Fleet Air Arm's stock in trade – fighter combat
expertise.

'In brief, we had to combine the flying
qualities of the machine with tactical procedures
that were based on the particular characteristics
of the aircraft in combat. These characteristics
are: low initial and sustained wingborne turn
rates; subsonic/transonic only; short-range
weapon system (guns, AIM-9, Magic); forgiv-

ing handling in wingborne flight; terrific deceleration; small size; smoke-free exhaust; low fuel consumption at high power equals persistence; and outstanding low-speed man-oeuvrability.

'The table below depicts where the Sea Harrier's characteristics differ from those of the USAF's F-15 Eagle. In the glossy brochure areas (speed and turn rates) the F-15 is without question the superior aircraft and I choose it to make comparisons for a particular reason.

	Sea Harrier	F-15
Turn rate	–	+
Speed	–	+
Weapon system	–	+
Forgiving handling	Equal	
Deceleration	+	–
Size	+	–
Exhaust visibility	+	–
Fuel consumption	+	–
Low-speed manoeuvre	+	–

'During the early months of service, I arranged for us to take a detachment of three aircraft to visit the USAF Aggressor Squadron at RAF Alconbury. The Aggressors fly the F-5E and their sole purpose of life is to train USA and NATO fighter squadrons in the art and tactics of fighter combat. To this end they are staffed with hand-picked aviators who are no slouches in combat. Naturally, they provide an ideal testing ground for any aircraft and tactics.

'So it proved. At the end of the first day of one-versus-one combat, the F-5 Aggressor pilots were wondering what had hit them. They actually asked if we had been sent down to

evaluate them! Our kill ratio against them turned out to be better than three to one, my own score being twelve kills and one lost.

'Within days of returning to base, I had a call from the USAF F-15 squadron at Bitburg, Germany: "Can we come over and fight you?" Of course, the answer was yes, and within a week we were hosting a flight of F-15s and conducting four sorties of two-versus-two air-to-air combat.

'At this stage of the Sea Harrier's life, the radar had not been delivered and one would have expected the F-15, with its full weapon system of Sparrow, Sidewinder and guns, to "whitewash" us. Interestingly though, not a single Sparrow kill was achieved, and seven out of the eight first kills went to the Sea Harrier! Each flight progressed from that point and, during the subsequent dog-fighting the honours were about even.

'We have fought the F-15 and the Aggressors many times since that occasion, mainly on fully instrumented air combat ranges (such as Decimomannu), and the accredited kill rate has always been about three to one in the Sea Harrier's favour. Similar success rates have been achieved against every fighter we have faced. For example, at least ten to one against the Phantom and about two to one against the F-16.

'The table below gives an overall summary of our experiences with the Sea Harrier in air combat engagements (the kill ratio is Sea Harrier wins against adversary wins).

The first two-seat Harrier attached to the Royal Navy was an RAF T.4, XW927, but at a later date Sea Harrier pilots were able to convert on the Navy's own T.4Ns.

The second production Sea Harrier (above right), XZ451, carrying the tail markings of No. 700A Intensive Flying Trials Unit. When this photograph was taken, in April 1980, No. 700A had already disbanded and re-formed as No. 899 Headquarters and Training Squadron.

A Sea Harrier of No. 700A Squadron carrying out deck landing operations on board the carrier HMS Hermes.

Venue	Adversary	Kill ratio
Decimomannu 1981	F-15 and F-5E	12:4
Decimomannu 1983	F-16	31:14
Alconbury	F-5E	3:1
NATO sea exercise	F-14	3:1–10:1
UK	F-4	10:1
Australia	Mirage III	3:1
UK	Lightning	2:1

'Why should the Sea Harrier be so successful in combat when its brochure figures look so ordinary? One clue to this lies in the slightly better performance of the F-16 over the F-15 when opposed by the Sea Harrier. Another is the ability of the fighter to see the target on radar initially and then to retain visual contact during fully fledged combat within visual range. The Sea Harrier is difficult if not impossible to keep track of visually beyond three nautical miles range. The F-15 on the other hand is easy to see at more than seven nautical miles range. The F-16 is less conspicuous than the F-15, being slightly smaller – hence its better combat performance against the Sea Harrier.

'However, once the engagement becomes visual, and with their superior turn and speed performance, one would expect the F-15/F-16 types of fighter to do better. Unfortunately for them, turn rate and speed are of secondary importance if you are being "pointed" by your adversary and his weapon system.

'The Sea Harrier "points" remarkably well at slow speed. The nose can be sliced in yaw (as opposed to being pitched) at greater rates than the sustained turn rate of either F-15 or F-16, but to do this speed has to be low. Fortunately, the Sea Harrier can attain low speed very quickly using nozzle and manoeuvre, point its nose at the target and then accelerate adequately quickly to get out of trouble. In this regime it is arguably the most agile fighter in the world, although the F-18, at vastly greater expense, may be able to equal it. The F-18 suffers disadvantages in other areas which tend to cancel out its "brochure" advantages.

'The success of the Harrier and, in particular, the Sea Harrier in combat rests not only in the aircraft's handling and performance characteristics. Undoubtedly these are important, and the Sea Harrier pilot will never be able to reach his peak unless he masters his handling of the aircraft throughout its performance envelope. However, of equal if not more importance to success is the need for the pilot to be a first class tactician and weapon system handler.

'One measure of excellence in the design of a

A No 700A Squadron Sea Harrier practises deck-landing aboard *Hermes*.

pilot/weapon system interface is that is should represent low pilot workload, whether measured in time or in level of concentration required. On entry into service the Sea Harrier was blessed with state-of-the-art avionics which had been programmed to satisfy just these criteria. During these trials, some minor deficiencies arose but were soon resolved, leaving the operator with a "user-friendly" system that required relatively little training and little natural aptitude for radar/computer operations.

'The system was by no means a hands-on-throttle-and-stick (HOTAS) system and, strangely enough, it was in the dog-fight environment that the system left most to be desired. This was because the selection and control of the weapons took too much time and necessitated taking one's concentration away from the fight.

'Nevertheless, in all other applications the avionics were easy to handle and reliable, and they performed well up to the design specification, as of course did the aircraft. It may interest you to know that the AV-8A Harrier is held in the highest regard by the US Marine Corps because "it is the only aircraft we have bought that has lived up to the glossy brochure in an operational environment".'

During weapon system trials and major exercises at sea between 1980 and 1982, the Sea Harrier had already convinced its operators (the aircrew and maintainance engineers) of its value. In spite of much bureaucratic opposition – there were those who thought it would never be adequate for all-weather night operations – the aircraft excelled in every major NATO exercise in which it took part and exceeded the hopes of every fleet commander in four principal respects: it was always available for its tasked missions; it conducted those missions, whether air intercept, ship attack or reconnaissance, with first-class results; it was able to operate in weather that limits conventional carrier aircraft; and it was entirely predictable as to its capability.

OPERATIONAL SQUADRONS

A second Sea Harrier squadron, No. 800, was commissioned on 23 April 1980, and was followed by No. 801 Squadron on 26 February 1981. The planned peacetime establishment of each squadron was five Sea Harriers: No 800

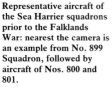

Representative aircraft of the Sea Harrier squadrons prior to the Falklands War: nearest the camera is an example from No. 899 Squadron, followed by aircraft of Nos. 800 and 801.

was to embark aboard HMS *Hermes*, forming a carrier air group with the Sea King ASW helicopters of No. 826 Squadron, while No. 801 was to go to HMS *Invincible* with No. 820 Squadron. Meanwhile, a second batch of ten Sea Harriers had been ordered from British Aerospace; the first of these, ZA174, flew on 15 September 1981 and was delivered to No. 899 Squadron.

Nos. 800 and 801 Squadrons both had reputations to uphold. Both had been formed originally in April 1933 with the amalgamation of the Fleet Air Arm's fighter flights and had gone to sea aboard the aircraft carriers *Courageous* and *Furious* respectively, No. 800 subsequently transferring to the newly commissioned *Ark Royal* in 1938. Both units served as naval fighter squadrons throughout the Second World War, covering every theatre of operations, and had seen action in Korea. No.

801 Squadron later disbanded, but No. 800 became the Fleet Air Arm's first jet fighter unit, equipping with Supermarine Attackers in 1951 and later operating with Scimitars. In 1964, it became the third squadron to equip with the Buccaneer, having been preceded by Nos. 801 and 809 Squadrons – the units which, together with No. 899, were to join forces in the South Atlantic struggle almost two decades later.

If anyone, particularly the Americans, felt sceptical about the Sea Harrier's ability to cope in an environment dominated by supersonic, carrier-borne fighters, such doubts were quickly dispelled in the course of a series of NATO exercises held in the North Atlantic during the late summer of 1981. In August, five Sea Harriers of 801 Squadron embarked aboard *Invincible* at Norfolk, Virginia, to form the strike element of the carrier's Air Group, which also comprised nineteen Sea King helicopters.

HMS *Hermes* and her Air Group – Sea Harriers of No. 800 Squadron and Sea King ASW helicopters of No. 826 Squadron.

A close-up view of a
development Sea Harrier
at the hover during carrier
trials.

A Sea Harrier FRS.1
showing the position of the
flight refuelling probe.

A Sea Harrier FRS.1 over Yeovilton (above left).

Sea Harriers of No. 801 Squadron (HMS *Invincible*) formate off the coast of Portugal during Exercise 'Ocean Safari' (above right). (Royal Navy)

Sea Harrier FRS.1s of Nos. 800, 801 and 899 Naval Air Squadrons.

The carrier was tasked to take part in Exercise 'Ocean Venture' which consisted of two opposing forces and took in a route from Norfolk across the Atlantic, through the Iceland–Faroes Gap and up to Norway. The task of *Invincible* and her Air Group, together with other escorting vessels, was to defend the giant 90,000-ton carrier USS *Dwight D. Eisenhower* against attacks by other forces, including Royal Canadian Navy ships as well as submarines and aircraft; in addition, the opposition had the support of another large carrier, USS *Forrestal*, with her complement of F-14s. A total of 70 ships took part.

This was the *Invincible*'s first major test with the Sea Harriers of No. 801 Squadron, and the ship and her aircraft were watched closely to evaluate their combined performance. No one was disappointed, and many were agreeably surprised by the effectiveness of the latest addition to the Royal Navy. The ship's performance as a unit was suitably described by the battle group's Commander, Rear Admiral J. Tuttle of the US Navy: 'It was the finest anti-submarine protection I have ever seen in my entire career,' he commented, and added about the British commander, Rear Admiral J. Cox,

'Cox made those goddam aircraft do things that surprised me. I was impressed.' Captain E. Clexton of the *Dwight D. Eisenhower* echoed these sentiments when he said, 'In the whole exercise there was not a single submarine from my nation – and that included the Russians if they were around – who got near enough to have taken a shot at us.' The submarine 'attacks' were not made singly. At one point during the exercise, *Invincible* was tracking at least three nuclear-powered submarines and a number of conventional ones as well as she swept ahead of the *Dwight D. Eisenhower*, clearing the way for her larger consort.

While the ship was engaged in her anti-submarine role, the Sea Harriers were also fully occupied in air defence sorties against F-14s from *Forrestal*, and, to add a touch of realism, Russian 'Bear' aircraft attempting to shadow the battle group were frequently intercepted by No. 801 Squadron. During the peak of operations, No. 801 maintained continuous air patrols for a total of 90 hours. This involved one aircraft on patrol, one on readiness with the pilot in the cockpit and a third aircraft on stand-by.

Following Exercise 'Ocean Venture', and with only a five-day gap, the ship and squadron

Sea Harriers of No. 800 Squadron, HMS *Hermes*. The normal fixed-wing complement of the carrier's peacetime Air Group comprised five aircraft.

Sea Harriers of No 801 Squadron, *Invincible*, during Exercise 'Ocean Safari'.

repeated their performance in a second major exercise, 'Ocean Safari', which consisted of convoy escort duties from the UK to Portugal and back again in the face of units from other navies with anti-submarine and air interception missions. The Sea Harriers performed superbly throughout the entire operation, with all aircraft remaining serviceable. Minor repairs and servicing were completed without any difficulties and with a rapid turn-round, leaving the squadron free to carry out its intercept missions. The Sea Harrier squadron began its night flying missions very early on in the exercises and completed well over 100 night deck landings, bringing both pilots and aircraft to all-weather operational capability. In addition, No. 801 Squadron carried out several non-diversionary night landings. During both exercises, the Sea

Harriers carried guns, Sidewinders and drop tanks for their interceptor roles.

During 1981, following a 'showing the flag' visit to the USA, the other Sea Harrier squadron, No. 800, operated in exercises with the carrier *Forrestal*. Air Group squadron commanders from that ship visited HMS *Hermes*, and were very impressed by both the serviceability of the aircraft and the high sortie rates. During the passage from Europe, No. 800 regularly achieved four sorties per pilot a day, and the general impression was that this could have been improved upon with at least two more pilots.

This early combat training under realistic conditions and in all kinds of weather was to stand Nos. 800 and 801 Naval Air Squadrons in good stead during real combat in 1982.

Sea Harriers of Nos. 800 and 899 Squadrons share the flight line with USMC AV-8A Harriers during a visit by the latter to RNAS Yeovilton. See also previous spread. (Royal Navy)

At 04.00hrs on 2 April 1982, Lt. Cdr. Andrew Auld, Officer Commanding No. 800 Squadron, was contacted by the Flag Officer Naval Air Command's staff at RNAS Yeovilton and told to bring his unit to immediate readiness. Despite the fact that No. 800 was due to go on leave, the call came as no surprise to Auld: he had been half expecting it ever since Argentinian scrap dealers had refused to leave South Georgia. Now the word had come that Argentinian forces had invaded the Falkland Islands themselves, and

the machinery was being set in motion to assemble the British Task Force that would repossess them. Similar orders were also issued to Lt. Cdr. Nigel Ward of No. 801 Squadron and Lt. Cdr. Tony Ogilvy of No. 899 Headquarters and Training Squadron. Most of the personnel of No. 801 had already departed on leave and were now the subject of an urgent recall. All three squadrons were equipped with the British Aerospace Sea Harrier FRS.1.

Politics apart, the actual events which had led

HMS *Hermes* en route for the Falklands with her Air Group of eleven Sea Harriers and six Sea King helicopters. Shortly after leaving Portsmouth on 5 April 1982, she was joined by another Sea Harrier, bringing No. 800 Squadron's strength, supplemented by No. 899 Squadron, to twelve aircraft.

to the mobilization of Task Force 317 had begun just prior to Argentina's invasion of the Falkland Islands and South Georgia. Admiral John Fieldhouse GCB GBE, subsequently overall commander of the Task Force, had received orders on 31 March to make covert preparations. Admiral Fieldhouse had just returned from the Mediterranean where the Royal Navy had been taking part in Exercise 'Springtrain'. Before leaving Gibraltar, he had ordered the Flag Officer First Flotilla, Rear Admiral John (Sandy) Woodward, at that time the most junior of the Royal Navy's three sea-going admirals, to prepare to detach a suitable group of ships to store ammunition and to be ready to proceed to the South Atlantic. On 29 March, the nuclear-powered submarine HMS *Spartan* was detached from Exercise 'Springtrain' and ordered to embark stores and weapons at Gibraltar for

deployment to the South Atlantic. The following day, a second submarine, HMS *Splendid*, was ordered to deploy from Faslane, and a third, HMS *Conqueror*, sailed a few days later. All were stored within 48 hours. A total of five nuclear-powered submarines, referred to as Task Force 324, were deployed during the campaign, operating under the direct control of Naval HQ at Northwood.

The morning of 2 April witnessed a scene of incredible bustle and activity at Yeovilton as the Sea Harrier squadrons with all their associated personnel and stores prepared to embark on the vessels that would take them to the South Atlantic. By 16.00hrs, No. 800 Squadron was embarked on board the aircraft carrier *Hermes* with eight Sea Harriers, three of which in fact belonged to No. 899. For the remainder of the weekend all personnel helped store ship, officers

HMS *Invincible* setting out from Portsmouth. The Sea Harrier on the ski-jump is an aircraft of No. 899 Squadron.

and ratings alike joining the long lines of men who were passing tons of stores aboard to be packed in every available area. During the weekend, *Hermes* received another three Sea Harriers, bringing the strength up to eleven. Shortly after leaving Portsmouth on 5 April, she was joined by the last Sea Harrier, bringing No. 800 Squadron's strength, supplemented by No. 899, to twelve aircraft operated by sixteen pilots, three air engineering officers and 154 ratings.

Meanwhile, No. 801 Squadron, which had taken somewhat longer to recall because the unit was on leave, had begun to embark on the carrier *Invincible*, the squadron's own five Sea Harriers being joined by three from No. 899 Squadron. After storing ship to the levels necessary to support an extended deployment 8,000 miles away, *Hermes* and *Invincible* sailed with their escorts on Monday 5 April 1982.

FORMING A FOURTH SQUADRON

One naval officer well aware of the Sea Harrier's capabilities was Lt. Cdr. Tim Gedge, who had only recently handed over command of the first front-line Sea Harrier unit, No. 800 Squadron, to Auld prior to taking up a staff post. Shortly after watching the carriers sail southwards from Portsmouth on 5 April, Gedge was contacted by the Flag Officer Naval Air Command and ordered to form another front-line Sea Harrier unit. Initially, the task was to recommence the training 'pipeline' and also to provide a reserve of pilots and aircraft for the South Atlantic operation.

On 6 April, Gedge arrived at Yeovilton and began to set about the complicated task of raising a squadron of ten aircraft – twice the size of the normal peacetime Sea Harrier unit. It posed many problems at first, not least obtaining the aircraft and ensuring that they would be fully equipped and ready for war. In addition, there was the major question of who would fly them: Sea Harrier pilots were few in number and spread far and wide. Those on exchange appointments in the USA and Australia were immediately brought home, while others within the UK were brought back to Yeovilton.

The aircraft that were available were in several stages of refit or repair, or still under construction at the factory. Once Gedge's team had managed to hasten them through their programmes and get very early deliveries from

British Aerospace, who managed to complete aircraft well ahead of schedule, they began to consider what colour the paint scheme should be. They knew already that the squadrons at sea in the *Hermes* and *Invincible* had repainted their aircraft, but beyond that they were treading new ground.

It was at this stage that the team brought in an expert from the Royal Aircraft Establishment at Farnborough who had investigated the typical weather conditions of the Falklands area for that time of year and advised them to paint the aircraft in the colour that would blend in most suitably with the prevailing background – light grey. It is interesting that the final colour adopted by the Fleet Air Arm for their Sea Harriers after the Falklands campaign was slightly darker than the one chosen by No. 809 Squadron, and a slightly lighter grey than the one in which the other units had painted their aircraft while going south in the carriers. The reason for the lack of uniformity in the grey paint schemes adopted by the squadrons en route for the Falklands was that the paint stocks available on board *Invincible* and *Hermes* were not standard colours.

During the three weeks that followed, an enormous amount of work was done at Yeovilton, including gathering the aircraft together. The Sea Harriers had to be totally complete for war and the problems of acquiring equipment were very great. It was an incredible effort, not only from within the service, but also from industry. Finally, on 20 April, No. 809 Squadron was declared operational with eight fully equipped Sea Harriers. It was short of the number Gedge wanted, but two had to be left behind to form the nucleus of a training programme at Yeovilton. Whatever was happening to the front-line squadrons down south, it was important to continue training and development as far as possible.

Some difficulty was also experienced in obtaining the required number of pilots for the eight aircraft. There were six Royal Navy pilots, but two more still had to be found, and Royal Navy personnel sources were exhausted, except for those who were to stay behind and continue the task at home. The solution adopted by No. 809 was to look for two RAF Harrier pilots with current experience but who had also had Lightning interceptor experience, thus providing the best option for a very quick conversion. Fortunately, both were found quickly, flying

The pilots of the newly reformed No. 809 Squadron practise some immaculate formation flying prior to their departure from the UK. The Squadron's personnel included two RAF pilots posted from the Harrier squadrons in Germany.

The crest of No. 809 Squadron, a phoenix rising from the flames, shows up well against the grey paintwork of the unit's Sea Harriers.

with the Harrier squadrons in West Germany, and were posted rapidly to Yeovilton. During the next few days they were converted to the Sea Harrier, trained in the appropriate tactics, given some ski-jump launch practice at Yeovilton, and also taught how to use the Sea Harrier's radar – a daunting task for the men involved and one which they both tackled readily, achieving creditable results.

At last, No. 809 Squadron received the order to move: over a two-day period it was to ferry its aircraft to Ascension Island, refuelling in flight. Lt. Cdr. Gedge departed on the morning of Friday 30 April with two formations of three aircraft leaving an hour apart; the third flight, consisting of two aircraft, left Yeovilton the following day. Both of the original groups reached Ascension Island on 1 May, while the

third group arrived a day later. Each of the aircraft refuelled a total of fourteen times from RAF Victor tankers during the 9¼hr flight. The refuelling usually took the form of tanking two aircraft first and then the third. All the tanking went remarkably well and no problems were encountered, despite this being the first time that most of the pilots had refuelled the Sea Harrier in flight.

A Sea Harrier FRS.1 on the lift of HMS *Invincible*. The photograph was taken during trials.

TASK FORCE 317 WORK-UP

Returning to the Task Force itself, the Sea Harrier squadrons had been hard at work as the carriers progressed southwards, conducting a flying programme geared towards meeting the requirements of a campaign in the Falklands, working up a nucleus of experienced pilots and enabling the others to gain experience. One of the younger pilots had been taken from his Sea Harrier conversion course with less than thirty hours on type, while several others, although well-versed Harrier pilots, had only recently returned to Yeovilton to undergo refresher courses. All the new pilots quickly achieved a satisfactory standard of deck operations and the carriers worked up to intensive rates of flying operations – typically 40 Sea Harrier sorties per day in the case of *Hermes* – as well as operating anti-submarine routines and drills and flying the helicopters. By the time the Task Force arrived off Ascension Island, the pilots were in good flying practice in the attack role and had first-hand experience in the practical techniques of rendezvous and transit flying in large formations and in ship-attack profiles. Having sailed at action stations, the Task Force remained on a

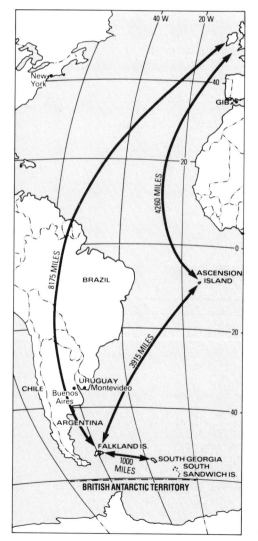

Sea Harrier XZ498 of No. 801 Squadron on the flight deck of HMS *Invincible*. The aircraft bears the name of Lt. Alan Curtis, who shot down an Argentine Air Force Canberra on 1 May but who, together with Lt. Cdr. John Eyton-Jones, failed to return to his ship five days later during a bad-weather sortie.

war footing, with the Sea Harriers maintaining a round-the-clock state of alert; in fact, a state of alert of one form or another was maintained by the Sea Harriers from that time until the Task Force once again reached Ascension on the way home.

Task Force 317 continued to make steady progress southwards from Ascension during mid-April. On the morning of the 21st, when

the Force was at position 19° 29′ south, 21° 0′ west, 1,430 miles east-north-east of Rio de Janeiro, radar picked up an airborne contact some 150 miles south of the warships and Lt. S. Hargreaves of No. 800 Squadron was ordered to investigate it. Initially, the contact was believed to be a commercial airliner, as several of these had come close to the Task Force during the preceding days, but as Hargreaves closed on the

Preparing a Sea Harrier for a sortie from HMS *Hermes* during the carrier's run southwards from Ascension Island.

target, which he identified as a Boeing 707, he saw the blue and white Argentine flag painted on its tail. It was, in fact, an aircraft of *Transport Grupo 1*, based at El Palomar, near Buenos Aires, and it had been sent out specifically to search for the Task Force. At this stage, negotiations were still going on at the United Nations to try to resolve the Falklands crisis by peaceful means, so Hargreaves, with strict instructions not to commit any warlike act, formated on the Boeing and photographed it with his fixed starboard-facing camera. Incursions by Argentine Air Force Boeing 707s became a daily occurrence from then on as they monitored the Task Force's progress, and the Sea Harrier squadrons maintained a continuous combat air patrol of two aircraft by day and one by night once the fleet reached latitude 35°S.

From the start, the primary role of both carriers was fleet air defence, but *Hermes*, with her large and varied magazine – 1,000lb bombs, cluster bombs and so on – was also tasked with a number of attack options against ship and land targets. Combat air patrols were carried out in increasing numbers each day as the Task Force came closer to the Falklands. CAPs were flown at between 60 and 80 miles from the British ships, and during the approach to the Total Exclusion Zone, a good deal of night flying was taking place. There was no accurate knowledge of what the Task Force would have to face inside the Zone and so, until the threat could be

quantified, exercises covered a wide range of tactical possibilities. New attack modes like 'loft' delivery were tried and live weapons were dropped to check arming and release circuits*.

---

*Loft delivery, used with laser target marking, resembles an underarm throw. The aircraft pulls up sharply into a climb and releases its bomb, which rises to about 500ft before curving down to the target.

Preparing Sea Harriers for launch prior to a strike mission from HMS Hermes.

OPERATIONAL BRIEF

In late April, and well south of Ascension Island, plans for an air attack on Port Stanley airfield were finalized. Lt. Cdr. Tony Ogilvy was responsible for working out the attack profile and, with a team to assist, produced the basic plan. In view of the intelligence reports of anti-aircraft artillery defences on and around the airfield, Ogilvy decided on two complementary attack profiles, using a total of nine aircraft. Four Sea Harriers would go in first to neutralize the anti-aircraft defences, closely followed by the remaining five, which would concentrate on dropping ordnance on to Stanley airfield. Accurate timing was essential for the attack to be effective and also to minimize the risk of losses. Three more Sea Harriers, under the command of Lt. Cdr. Frederiksen, were to hit the airstrip at Goose Green. All aircraft tasked with ground attack operations were to be launched from the *Hermes*, the *Invincible*'s Harriers being responsible for Task Force CAP.

At 04.46hrs, on Saturday 1 May, a stick of 1,000lb bombs dropped by a Vulcan of RAF Strike Command, operating out of Ascension Island on the longest-range bombing sortie in the history of air warfare, erupted across Port Stanley airfield. On completion of the operation, the Vulcan crew transmitted the codeword 'Superfuse'. The codeword was picked up by Task Force units moving into position a hundred miles ENE of the Falklands, in readiness to launch the planned attacks against the airstrips at Port Stanley and Goose Green. In the darkness before dawn, the Sea Harrier pilots boarded their aircraft. At 07.50hrs local time, as it was just beginning to get light, Lt. Cdr. Auld of No. 800 Squadron launched his aircraft from the ski-jump ramp. For the first time, a V/STOL combat aircraft was about to go into action. In the days to come, the British Aerospace Harrier would write a new chapter in the history of air warfare and would amply vindicate the confidence and dedication of all those who had fought so hard to bring the concept to fruition over more than two decades.

No. 800 SQUADRON: HMS *HERMES*

Lt. Cdr. Auld's force of twelve Sea Harriers formed up over HMS *Hermes* in the dawn twilight and set course west-south-west towards the Falkland Islands, flying at very low altitude. At 08.00 Port Stanley time, the three aircraft due to strike at Goose Green broke off and headed for their objective; five minutes later, the main force also split up, the four aircraft, led by Lt. Cdr. Tony Ogilvy of No. 899 Squadron, going into their bombing run while Auld led the remaining five into orbit to achieve separation.

Ogilvy's four Sea Harriers, each carrying three 1,000lb air-burst bombs, pulled up and released their ordnance, before turning sharply away to clear the Argentine defences around Port Stanley. The twelve bombs followed a 27-second trajectory before exploding above the enemy gun positions. Under cover of the confusion, Auld's five aircraft made their run across the airfield through heavy automatic weapons fire to lay down their cluster bombs and direct-action 1,000-pounders. Tigercat missiles were launched at the attackers, but with no result. Only the last Sea Harrier in the attack, flown by Flt. Lt. Dave Morgan RAF, sustained a hit – a 20mm cannon shell through the upper fin. All the aircraft involved in the Port Stanley attack recovered safely to *Hermes*, as did the three which attacked Goose Green. Lt. Cdr. R. Frederiksen and his pilots encountered limited small-arms fire, but they bombed and were away before the heavier defences had time to react.

The squadron's eleven serviceable Sea

Regular exercises in the arctic conditions of northern Norway stood the Sea Harrier squadrons in good stead for their operations in the South Atlantic winter. The photograph shows a Sea Harrier of No. 800 Squadron recovering after a simulated strike in support of forward troops.

A Sea Harrier of No. 809
Squadron, armed with
Sidewinders for CAP, is
marshalled on the flight
deck of HMS *Hermes*.

Royal Navy Sea Harriers
and Royal Air Force
Harrier GR.3s on board
HMS *Hermes*. During the
1982 war, Sea Harriers
concentrated on combat
air patrols, while RAF
Harriers carried out
ground attack missions in
support of British land
forces.

Harriers at once took on the fleet air defence role; the refuelling and rearming were so efficient that the first aircraft was launched only twenty minutes after it returned to the carrier from the attack sortie. Retaliation was anticipated, but none came; hostile aircraft were observed on radar to the west of the Task Force, but none ventured further east than the islands, where No. 801 Squadron had already had its first engagements.

The first contact for No. 800 came in the afternoon, when Flt. Lt. Bertie Penfold RAF, of No. 899 Squadron, and Lt. Martin Hale, flying Task Force CAP at 20,000ft, were attacked by Israeli-built IAI Daggers of the Argentine Air Force's *Grupo 6*. The Daggers were approaching from 12 o'clock high, at 30,000–35,000ft. One launched a Shafrir infrared homing missile that closed on Hale. He escaped by dumping chaff, carried behind the Sea Harrier's air brake, and diving into cloud at 5,000ft. Meanwhile Penfold, who had a visual on the Daggers, pulled up for a Sidewinder shot, his missile destroying the aircraft piloted by Lt. Jose Ardiles. It was the first Sea Harrier kill.

On 4 May, three Sea Harriers of No. 800 Squadron, led by Lt. Cdr. Gordon Batt, with Lt. Nick Taylor and Flt. Lt. Ted Ball, were launched to carry out a second attack on Goose Green. The preceding days had been quiet, shrouded in Falklands fog that had effectively halted flying operations. Lt. Cdr. Roger Bennett, No. 800's Engineering Officer, described the scene:

'It was an eerie and uncomfortable experience and an uneasy silence descended on us, broken only by the news of the sinking of the *General Belgrano*. During these fog-bound days – and there were many more to come – we maintained the aircraft on Alert 5, manned and ready to launch for defence. The pilots would sit in the cockpit, waiting for a couple of hours at a stretch.

'With the very poor visibility during these periods, I think the pilots were more than aware of the daunting prospect of landing back on board. It could so easily have been impossible and, if called, they could well have launched on a mission from which they could not have returned without wet feet, if they returned at all.

'Every dawn and dusk we went to action stations as standard routine because these times were considered the most likely for an attack.

A Sea Harrier launches from the ski-ramp of HMS *Hermes* to carry out a CAP sortie.

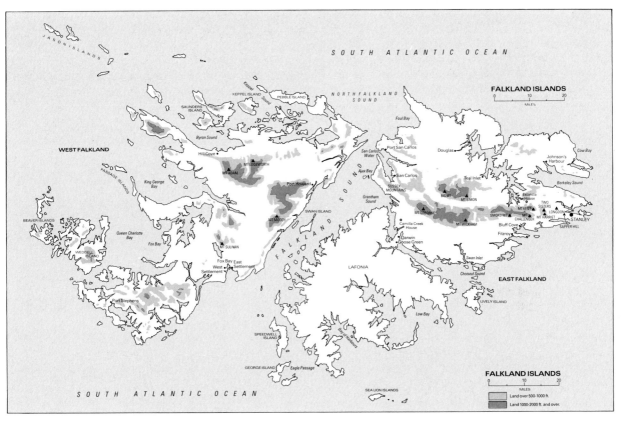

But as the days went by, we got to know the Argentines' pattern. They never attacked at dawn, always in the mid- or late afternoon and just before dusk.'

The three-aircraft attack on Goose Green on 4 May had a twofold objective: to crater the airstrip with three 1,000lb retarded bombs, which was Ted Ball's job, and to attack the airstrip's Pucara ground-attack aircraft with cluster bombs, which was the task of Batt and Taylor. During the strike, Nick Taylor's aircraft – XZ450, the first Sea Harrier to fly – was hit by what was probably 35mm Oerlikon fire, and burst into flames. It flew on for some distance before diving into the ground and exploding. The pilot did not survive.

The bad weather persisted, bringing a virtual halt to Sea Harrier operations. During the four-day period 5–8 May, No. 800 Squadron launched only four sorties, and on 9 May a planned high-level attack with 1,000lb bombs by Lt. Cdr. Batt and Flt. Lt. Morgan had to be abandoned because of cloud over the target. As they turned away, however, Morgan picked up a suspect surface contact on his radar and was

ordered to investigate by HMS *Coventry*, the control ship operating off the islands. The contact turned out to be the Argentine stern trawler *Narwal*. The Sea Harrier pilots received orders to engage her and attacked initially with their 1,000lb bombs, one of which lodged in the trawler's hull without exploding. They then strafed the vessel with their 30mm Aden cannon, causing damage to her engine room. She was later boarded by the Royal Navy and taken under tow, but she sank the next day.

Lt. Cdr. Bennett describes the next phase of operations:

'For the next two weeks, until the landing ships and troops arrived in numbers, we had to play a waiting game, and this period was a curious mixture of quiet interspersed with moments of furious activity.

'For much of this time, the fog came in again, bringing with it the infernal 100 per cent humidity. However, breaks in the weather allowed a certain amount of flying. . . . This relatively quiet interlude was interrupted with the news of the successful commando raid on Pebble Island, where a large number of Pucaras

A CAP pair of Sea Harriers recovering aboard HMS *Hermes*. The patrol has been uneventful, as is shown by the presence of both Sidewinders on each aircraft's wing pylons.

A Sea Harrier recovering to its carrier at dusk, with a Royal Fleet Auxiliary vessel in the background.

A post-Falklands photograph of a No. 800 Squadron Sea Harrier launching over the Atlantic (below left). The aircraft is carrying a Sidewinder training round.

were damaged. No. 800 Squadron continued regularly to bomb Stanley airfield to deny its use to fast jets, and at night the frigates and destroyers continued to provide a heavy shore bombardment to keep the defenders awake and generally demoralize them.'

No. 809 SQUADRON ARRIVES

Meanwhile, Harrier reinforcements were en route from Ascension Island. Lt. Tim Gedge of No. 809 Squadron takes up the story:

'We left Ascension Island on May 5. The *Atlantic Conveyor* was anchored a little way off the coast and we flew a short sortie from Wideawake airfield before recovering vertically on to the temporarily fitted vertical landing pad in the forward section of the ship. Aircraft were then parked between the two rows of containers, two-high, locked to the outer edges of the deck. These later provided some protection for the aircraft – without them, the Harriers and helicopters would have been exposed totally to the elements.

'We were very conscious of the need to keep the aircraft in pristine condition and though we washed them thoroughly at Ascension before our short hop they were again given a good washing once aboard *Atlantic Conveyor*. With us were six RAF Harrier GR.3s (No. 1 Squadron), which had also tanked out from the United Kingdom, four Chinook and six Wessex helicopters.

'Once aboard, most of the aircraft were covered with purpose-made, rubberized canvas bags. One Sea Harrier was kept permanently on alert, fuelled, armed and ready to be launched in the event of the ship being intercepted by an Argentine aircraft. A second Sea Harrier was kept as a back-up.

'While on passage – it took twelve days to reach the Task Force – we carried out some minor work on the aircraft, including completing the new radio installations. The most was made of these non-flying days by holding discussions and briefings on the tactics we would use and which we knew would figure in our future operations. The opportunity was taken to get to know the pilots of No. 1 (Fighter) Squadron and joint briefings were held. Most of them were travelling aboard the North Sea ferry *Norland*, which was sailing in company with the *Atlantic Conveyor*, and they transferred over to us on occasion, by helicopter. On May 19, we began transferring the Harriers from *Atlantic Conveyor* to the carriers. Four of No. 809's aircraft were to operate from HMS *Hermes*, and four from *Invincible*. All the RAF Harrier GR.3s were taken aboard *Hermes*.'

The extra aircraft now brought *Hermes*' total complement up to 21. Some extra maintenance personnel also arrived, including seventeen from the RAF, and this increased No. 800 Squadron's total manpower to 180 – a ratio of less than nine men for each aircraft; the peacetime ratio was twenty men per aircraft. The biggest problem was that there were still only sixteen armourers, who had to attend to an extra ten aircraft. A reduced schedule wartime servicing system was in use, and its successful operation became crucial with the increased workload.

On 21 May, an amphibious landing was made at San Carlos. The landing ships, merchantmen and the troopship *Canberra*, under the protec-

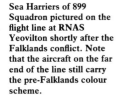

Sea Harriers of 899 Squadron pictured on the flight line at RNAS Yeovilton shortly after the Falklands conflict. Note that the aircraft on the far end of the line still carry the pre-Falklands colour scheme.

tion of frigates and destroyers, went inshore overnight, leaving *Hermes, Invincible* and a few escorts well to the east to provide air cover. Sea Harriers were launched on CAP at the rate of a pair every 20 minutes to provide non-stop cover near the landing area, having now been released from their ground-attack mission by the arrival of the Harrier GR.3s. After leaving their respective carriers, the Sea Harriers usually came under the tactical control of the screening warships, usually Type 42 destroyers and, occasionally, Type 22 frigates, but much of the interception work was autonomous, with the Sea Harriers on CAP, picking up the raids as they came in at low level.

Lt. Cdr. Tony Ogilvy, of No. 899 Squadron, was full of praise for the air defence ships in the San Carlos area: 'HMS *Brilliant*, in particular, deserves a special mention. Whilst under heavy attack herself, the First Lieutenant, using the ship's radar, directed Sea Harrier patrols on to raids approaching to attack at very low level. Anything I can say would never do justice to the bravery and dedication shown by those ships and their crews in the Sound.'

It was HMS *Brilliant* which, early in the afternoon of 21 May, directed Lt. Cdrs. Neil Thomas and Mike Blissett of No. 800 Squadron, who were just arriving on CAP over Falkland Sound, to intercept an A-4 Skyhawk which had attacked the frigate HMS *Ardent*. Instead, they sighted four Skyhawks, crossing from left to right, about three miles away over the coast. The enemy aircraft were engaged from astern and two were shot down with Sidewinders; the two survivors were engaged with 30mm cannon fire, but escaped when the Sea Harriers were compelled to break contact, short of fuel.

At about 14.30hrs, *Brilliant* directed a new No. 800 Squadron CAP pair, Lt. Cdr. Frederiksen and Lt. Andrew George, to intercept four IAI Daggers over West Falkland. Frederiksen hit the rear aircraft with a Sidewinder and it went down to crash, the pilot ejecting. He fired his cannon at a second Dagger, but it escaped into cloud, along with the other two. A few minutes later, a third CAP pair from No. 800 Squadron, Lt. Clive Morell and Flt. Lt. John Leeming, were called down to engage three Skyhawks attacking *Ardent*. The two Sea Harrier pilots saw the enemy bombs exploding near the warship, and almost immediately sighted the Skyhawks, which were easy to see

Previous spread: Formation flying by No 809 Squadron.

The container ship *Atlantic Conveyor* as she appeared when she joined the Task Force. Captain North, her master, had ordered that the ship's superstructure should be painted overall grey, an exercise in camouflage that was only partly completed at this stage.

Running low on fuel when the temporary landing strip at San Carlos was damaged, this Sea Harrier of No. 800 Squadron diverted to HMS *Intrepid*.

because of their glossy white paintwork. Morell launched a Sidewinder at the lead aircraft and severely damaged it around the tail unit, compelling the pilot, Lt. Cdr. Philippi of *Grupo 5*, to eject. Morell locked on to a second Skyhawk but had some difficulty launching his other AIM-9L, and when it finally did launch it failed to guide properly, dropping away into the sea. Meanwhile Flt. Lt. Leeming had engaged the rearmost Skyhawk with 30mm cannon fire: after three sighting bursts the enemy aircraft rolled away to starboard and literally fell apart in a cloud of debris as Leeming's fourth burst struck it. Later, it was established that the third

A fine photograph of HMS Broadword, taken from HMS Invincible. Broadswood, equipped with highly effective Seawolf surface-to-air missiles, was one of the vessels detailed to act as 'goalkeeper' for the all-important carriers throughout the Falklands conflict.

Skyhawk – the one that had evaded Morell's missile – had come down in the sea, damaged by fire from the warships and possibly from a burst of 30mm Morell had sent after it. The pilot, Lt. Arca, was picked up after ejecting.

No. 800 Squadron made no further contact with the enemy that day, but early on 22 May Lt. Cdr. Frederiksen and Lt. Martin Hale strafed an Argentine patrol boat, the *Rio Iguazu*, that was attempting to run in supplies to the garrison at Choiseul Sound and left it burning. It was later beached and abandoned.

The Squadron's next action, on 23 May, was a joint RAF affair. Flt. Lts. Dave Morgan and

John Leeming were flying CAP at 8,000ft over Falkland Sound when Morgan spotted what appeared to be a helicopter flying over an inlet. It was an Argentine Army Puma. As the two Sea Harriers closed in, they saw two more Pumas and an Agusta 109, all following the first in line astern. Morgan pulled over the leading helicopter, intending to turn and get into firing position, and it suddenly went down and crashed, the pilot either losing control through Morgan's slipstream or in the process of taking evasive action. Meanwhile, the Agusta had landed and been abandoned by its crew, so the Sea Harrier pilots strafed it and set it on fire. One of the Pumas had also landed further up the valley, and this too was strafed by Morgan and Leeming before they departed.

That afternoon, at about 16.00hrs, Lt. Cdr. Auld and Lt. Martin Hale of No. 800 Squadron were flying CAP when Hale sighted a Dagger flying west at high speed. He gave chase but was unable to catch the enemy aircraft, but a moment later he sighted a second Dagger and closed for a Sidewinder engagement from astern, launching from half a mile. The missile struck home and the Dagger exploded over Horseshoe Bay. Later that day, No. 800 Squadron experienced its second loss of the Falklands

War when Sea Harrier ZA192 crashed on take-off from *Hermes*, killing its pilot, Lt. Cdr. Gordon Batt DSC. The Sea Harrier was one of four tasked with a strike on Port Stanley airfield.

At first light on 24 May, two Sea Harriers of No. 800 Squadron, flown by Lt. Cdrs. Neil Thomas and Mike Blissett, carried out a toss-bombing attack on Port Stanley airfield, preceding a lay-down attack by four Harrier GR.3s of No. 1 Squadron, using 1,000lb retarded bombs. Later that morning, Lt. Cdr. Andy Auld and Lt. Dave Smith were on CAP off Pebble Island when the frigate HMS *Broadsword* vectored them on to a hostile radar contact. Smith, going into his first combat, describes what happened:

'We had just arrived in the zone when we received an "area warning red" call from HMS *Broadsword* which was on radar picket duty. Using her pulse doppler radar, she had picked up incoming aircraft and we were called in to intercept. We were flying up at 10,000 feet at the time and were vectored to 260 degrees, diving down to the surface at high speed. I slammed open the throttle and tucked myself in behind the Boss, about 100 yards away. As we passed through 550 knots, we were down to about 150

A Sea Harrier recovering
to its carrier at the end of
a sortie.

Turning round a Sea
Harrier between sorties. A
very high sortie rate was
maintained by the Sea
Harrier squadrons at peak
periods during the
Falklands conflict.

A Sea Harrier of No. 800 Squadron on *Hermes'* flight deck, with *Broadsword* and *Invincible* in the background. This sea state was typical of the conditions prevailing in the South Atlantic at the time of the Falklands War. (Royal Navy)

A Sea Harrier of No. 801 Squadron recovers aboard *Invincible*.

A Sea Harrier recovers
aboard HMS *Hermes*.

feet and began a hard turn towards the rapidly
approaching enemy. Suddenly the Boss called
"visual" and there they were – four Mirages
coming in very low and very fast. [In fact, they
were Daggers of *Grupo 6*. Author.]

'As I picked them up, the Boss rolled in
behind and fired both his Sidewinders in quick
succession – both hit and two Mirages exploded
in violent fireballs. The second pair broke hard
right and I locked on to one of them. As I did so
I saw him bang off his tanks and bombs to
improve his manoeuvrability. As my missile
"cross" flashed across his tail, I heard the
acquisition "growl" of the Sidewinder in my
headset. I pressed the lock button, released the
safety catch and fired. Fractions of a second
later there was a flash from under my wing as the
Sidewinder leapt off its pylon rails.

'At first I thought I had missed, as the
Sidewinder shot off to the right and was not
heading towards the Mirage. What was not
immediately apparent though was that the
Sidewinder had already worked out the interception angle and was off-cutting the corner to
reach the Mirage. Sure enough, as the Mirage
was moving across my front from left to right,
the Sidewinder zeroed in on his hot tail pipe and
hit him.

'There was another flash and a fireball with
the Mirage breaking up and impacting the
ground in a burning inferno. It was an incredible sight. In less than five seconds we had
destroyed three enemy aircraft. Now for the
fourth, but where was he? Suddenly I saw him
under the Boss, heading west at high speed. As I
still had one Sidewinder left, we turned hard
and followed him. We were both going flat out
for some minutes, with me just out of missile
range. But we were by then getting low on fuel
so we had to break off, but we heard later that he
too had run out of fuel and had to ditch on his
return home.'

On 25 May, Argentina's National Day,
Argentine aircraft launched a series of heavy
attacks on the British beach-head at San Carlos
Water. The Sea Harriers of No. 800 Squadron
were once more flying CAP over the area, but
the pilots experienced moments of bitter
frustration as they either arrived over the beach-
head just as an Argentine raid was leaving or had
to leave themselves owing to their fuel state just
as another raid was building up. To cope with
this, the Task Force commander moved his
carriers west to within 130 miles of the landing
area to increase CAP time. However, there were

still problems: for example, on more than one occasion Sea Harriers had to break off an interception when they ran the risk of entering a friendly missile engagement zone. The Sea Harriers scored no air combat successes on 25 May, a day that cost the Task Force the Type 42 destroyer HMS *Coventry* and the container ship *Atlantic Conveyor*.

Every day, on board HMS *Hermes*, No. 800 Squadron was running a programme that often required up to ten Sea Harriers at any one time. All this, with aircraft on alert throughout the night, was a tremendous task for the pilots involved, particularly the night team. At the height of the air battle they would spend up to ten hours out of 24 in the cockpit, either flying or at alert. By now the great strength of the Sea Harrier was becoming apparent: under operational conditions, the aircraft and its systems were holding up beyond anyone's expectations. Of the sixteen Sea Harriers on board HMS *Hermes*, at least ten were serviceable at any one time. 'During the time that I was embarked,' recalls Lt. Cdr. Ogilvy of No. 899 Squadron, 'not one Sea Harrier needed an engine change. But I think, most important of all, the aircraft *worked* so well in all roles. Every Sidewinder launched correctly; not once did the Aden guns fail; and all bombs separated properly fused and they all functioned. The avionics held up well, with few spares needed, and even with a very occasional degraded weapon system, missiles and bombs still hit their targets. The F95 reconnaissance camera did not let us down and the aircraft showed that it can take battle damage.'

At one period, HMS *Hermes* was flying 40 Harrier sorties a day, at times in appalling weather – less than 200ft cloud base and well under half a mile visibility – and in sea states that only the South Atlantic can provide. Harrier recoveries came in to the deck from all angles – over the bows, up the wake and over the stern, from port or from starboard – with touchdowns amidships, on the afterdeck and just behind the bow ski-jump. Because of the ever-present threat of hostile submarines, the Admiral preferred to steam the Task Force at 15kts or so, and it would have been tactically very unsound to turn the carrier into wind for every launch and recovery as would have have been necessary with a flat-top operating conventional naval jets.

After 25 May, there were no air actions for several days. Some attempts were made to intercept Argentine aircraft by CAP Sea Harriers, but the enemy used his superior speed to escape. Losses sustained by the Argentines during this period were caused by surface-to-air missiles and small-arms fire.

On 31 May, troops of the 5th Infantry Brigade arrived at San Carlos to consolidate the bridgehead and prepare for the breakout and advance on Port Stanley. At the same time, a forward operating base (FOB) for the Harriers was assembled and constructed by Nos. 11 and 59 Squadrons, Royal Engineers, at Port San Carlos. It consisted of an 850ft strip of aluminium MEXE matting, with holding and refuelling loops at one end. The site was ready for operations on 5 June, and No. 800 Squadron provided the first Sea Harriers to land there. The effect on CAP operations was dramatic: a Sea Harrier launched from *Hermes* could remain on task for an indefinite period by refuelling at this forward base, as long as weapons were not expended and the aircraft remained serviceable. The strip, quaintly named HMS *Sheathbill*, was subsequently used many times, and it was not unusual to find six Sea Harriers there at any one time. Pilots encountered no problems in translating from ship to shore operations and back again, and on one occasion the nearby landing ships *Fearless* and *Intrepid* were used for refuelling purposes. The aircraft landed vertically and took on enough fuel from the two ships to get them back to the carrier.

No. 800 Squadron's last air action of the Falklands War took place on 8 June, the day the Royal Fleet Auxiliary logistics ships *Sir Galahad* and *Sir Tristram* were bombed at Fitzroy with heavy loss of life. Flt. Lt. Morgan and Lt. Smith were on CAP at 10,000ft in the area, and Smith describes what happened:

'We could see the awful sight of the ships burning at Bluff Cove. The smoke was pouring out, thick and oily, and the entire after section of the ship [the *Sir Galahad*] was glowing red with the heat. It was about 18.00hrs and getting dark when we noticed some Mirages having a go at some landing craft coming down from the direction of Goose Green. Dave [Morgan] rolled upside down and pulled hard for the surface. [In fact, the 'Mirages' were Skyhawks of *Grupo 5*; in the fading light, the mis-identification was understandable. Author.]

'I followed him down very fast, but he was nearly disappearing in the gloom. It was very hard to keep an eye on him. I slammed the

Two Sea Harriers of No. 800 Squadron recovering aboard *Hermes* after a CAP.

A Sea Harrier pictured at the moment of launch from HMS *Invincible*. The vessel in the background appears to be *Antrim*.

throttle to full power and aimed in the general direction in which Dave had by now disappeared. He must have been about half a mile ahead of me. My air speed was just over 600 knots when I saw two bright flashes from the direction of Dave's aircraft – he had fired both Sidewinders. I watched the white smoke trails and they ended in two fireballs as the Mirages disintegrated and hit the sea.

'Now where had he got to? Fortunately he opened up on the other two Mirages with his cannon and I just flew towards the shell splashes in the water – there he was. As I approached for an attack, Dave was in the way, but fortunately pulled out and cleared from my sights. I pointed the missile at the nearest bogey and heard the growl in my ears as the missile acquired him. I fired, thinking he was too far and going too fast for the missile to get him. The range was two or two-and-a-half miles, and as I watched the Sidewinder's trail it seemed to me that it flamed out about 300 yards short of its target. Evidently it did not, as there was a blinding flash, followed, fractions of a second later, by the Mirage impacting the ground.

'We could not stay around any longer as, again, our fuel states were getting low and we had to turn for home. We went up to high level for the long flight back to the carrier, and the recovery at the end of that was not particularly easy, being one of our first night landings.'

This final combat brought No. 800 Squadron's total of kills in the conflict to six Daggers and seven Skyhawks, together with one Islander, one Pucara, one Agusta 109 and one Puma destroyed on the ground. Another Puma, which flew into the ground as it was trying to evade attack, was also credited to the Squadron.

A Sea Harrier launches from *Hermes*. This photograph gives a good idea of the clutter and activity aboard the carriers during the Falklands operations.

No. 801 SQUADRON: HMS *INVINCIBLE*

No. 801 Squadron's war began before dawn on 1 May, when pairs of Sea Harriers were launched before the arrival of the RAF Vulcan from Ascension Island to provide cover in case of possible enemy fighter interception. Later, six Sea Harriers were launched to cover the attacks on Port Stanley and Goose Green by No. 800 Squadron's aircraft. No. 801's first real contact with the enemy came later that morning, when Lt. Cdr. Robin Kent and Lt. Brian Haigh engaged a pair of Mirage IIIs of *Grupo 8* north of the islands. The Mirages fired two missiles, which came nowhere near the Sea Harriers, and turned for home, still at high altitude. Later still, more Mirages were engaged by a second No. 801 Squadron pair, Lt. Cdr. John Eyton-Jones and Flt. Lt. Paul Barton. The Mirages once again fired their AAMs unsuccessfully and

the two Sea Harriers gave chase over West Falkland, but received so much ground fire from nearby Argentine defences that they were forced to break off.

At about midday it was the turn of No. 801 Squadron's commander, Lt. Cdr. 'Sharkey' Ward, to make contact with the enemy:

'My number two for this mission was Lieutenant Mike 'Soapy' Watson, fresh from Sea Harrier training but already a most professional operator. The day was beautifully clear with about half-cover of cloud over the island coastline between 800 and 2,500 feet. Our job was to protect a small group of our warships just north of the island [East Falkland], and excitement ran high in the cockpits when our control ship, HMS *Glamorgan*, reported three small aircraft contacts taking off from the runway at Port Stanley – so much for our hopes that the Vulcan raid had been successful!

The crowded flight deck of HMS *Hermes* seen at the close of the Falklands War, with RN Sea Harriers and RAF GR.3s ranged alongside one another.

'We were about 20 nautical miles from Stanley, turned towards it and began a rapid descent. Soapy immediately "taught his grand-dad new tricks" and acquired the enemy on radar close to the coast and heading north. We continued to close, penetrated the cloud cover and found three startled T-34s [Turbo-Mentors] just on the bottom edge of the cloud. They had seen us and immediately nosed up into the cloud, but not before we were close enough to take a longish-range potshot with guns. I pulled through the cloud in chase, passed too close for comfort to one T-34 and inverted to pull down below cloud again. They too emerged below but in complete disarray and, most importantly, jettisoning all their bombs and stores into the sea. Part of our aim was therefore achieved and our surface ships were safe.

'But at the time I was pretty disgusted with myself for missing with my initial cannon burst and spent the next two minutes trying to engage the enemy once more as they darted in and out through the clouds towards the coastline. They used the cloud well, survived, and my frustration was complete when I turned for safety as the last T-34 disappeared over the well-defended ridge just to the north of the airfield.

'Back on patrol together at medium altitude, we had little time for reflection. Three Mirages were reported to the south – approximately 40 miles and closing. Each time we vectored towards them they turned away, and so we decided to try to "spoof" them into combat. We flew north at a leisurely speed and medium altitude. Immediately *Glamorgan*'s commentary indicated that they had fallen for the spoof and had begun to close very rapidly. With the bait taken and the enemy fifteen miles astern, we turned hard into them and searched our radar screens avidly.

'Almost immediately three smoke trails appeared high in the sky ahead, coming directly towards us. Forsaking the radar, I attempted a visual missile lock on to the left-hand trail, and with a mixture of frustration and amusement realized my mistake – I was trying to track an air-to-air missile! Fortunately it ran out of steam before impact and oscillated its way into the sea below, as did the other two missiles. The Mirages had turned for home. It seemed as though the Argentine pilots had no desire to let us get to grips in close, and this was causing them to fire beyond the maximum effective range of their missiles.'

In the middle of the afternoon, another Sea Harrier CAP pair, Lt. Steve Thomas and Fl. Lt. Paul Barton, engaged two Mirages at close range. Thomas used his radar to control the Sea Harriers into firing positions and effectively drew the enemy's fire. The Mirages launched two AAMs, both of which missed. Barton then achieved a firing solution, launched the first AIM-9L Sidewinder of the war and saw his target explode in a ball of flame. Its pilot, Lt. Carlos Perona, ejected and survived. Thomas fired at a second Mirage, but as his missile closed on the target the latter entered cloud and he had no way of telling whether or not the kill had been achieved. In fact, the Mirage had been badly damaged by the Sidewinder, and its pilot, Capt. Garcia Cuerva, tried to make an emergency landing on the airstrip at Port Stanley. The aim of the Argentine gunners defending the airfield was better than their aircraft recognition: they shot Cuerva's aircraft down in flames, killing the luckless pilot.

As dusk was falling, Lt. Cdr. Mike Broadwater and Lt. Alan Curtis, working with No. 801 Squadron's fighter controller, intercepted three Canberras of *Grupo 2* which were inbound to strike the fleet. The controller, Lt. Bob Holmes, had a problem in that the enemy aircraft had approached at high level and then descended to low level some 100 miles from the Task Force, breaking ship's radar contact. Using his radar to good advantage, Curtis set up an autonomous interception in classic style, controlling his pair into a good firing position at very low level below cloud, and destroyed the lead Canberra with a Sidewinder shot. Both Argentine crew members ejected before the aircraft went down, but they were lost. Broadwater fired both his Sidewinders at one of the other evading Canberras, but neither missile impacted. Shortage of fuel then compelled the Sea Harriers to break off the action and return to *Invincible*.

There were no further air-to-air actions between 1 and 21 May, but during this period No. 801 Squadron suffered a sad loss when, on 6 May, Lt. Cdr. John Eyton-Jones and Lt. Alan Curtis, flying Sea Harriers XZ452 and XZ453, failed to return to *Invincible* after a CAP sortie in bad weather and in defence of the Task Force. The probable explanation is that the two aircraft collided. The companionship, experience and expertise of these two highly respected officers was to be sorely missed during the ensuing period, as aircrew fatigue set in and the flying programme remained the same. However, morale recovered rapidly and the Squadron's engineers continued to work their miracles with the reduced number of aircraft available.

Under cover of darkness on the night of 20–21 May, the amphibious group entered San Carlos Water and began to disembark 4,000 Royal Marines, soldiers and stores of all descriptions. This mammoth task was to last all day, and it was essential to protect both ships and personnel from loss. The amphibious force commander, Commodore Mike Clapp CB, achieved this protection in two ways. In a brilliant tactical move, he stationed seven warships outside San Carlos Water in the more open reaches of Falkland Sound. These frigates and destroyers were to form the second line of defence against the expected Argentine Air Force onslaught, the first line of defence being provided by the Sea Harrier CAPs.

That day, which cost the Argentine Air Force and Navy fifteen aircraft and helicopters, amply vindicated these tactics. Throughout the daylight hours, around 70 Daggers (erroneously described as Mirages by the CAP pilots) and Skyhawks penetrated the Sound, and many more than this number were turned away by the Sea Harrier cordon. One Skyhawk pilot who was shot down in the area shortly after 21 May admitted that he and his formation had been turned back on four separate occasions by Sea Harriers before eventually breaking through to attack the amphibious force.

Lt. Cdr. Ward had some pointed comments to make about the Sea Harrier operations during this crucial time:

'A considerable volume of uneducated comment has been made concerning the Sea Harrier's achievements in combat during this and other days of action. Much of the veiled or inferred criticism published in the Press, particularly by the French, has been in error. Both envy and commercial competitiveness

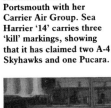

Hermes returns to Portsmouth with her Carrier Air Group. Sea Harrier '14' carries three 'kill' markings, showing that it has claimed two A-4 Skyhawks and one Pucara.

appear to have played a part in such criticism. One frequent comment has been that the enemy aircraft had too little fuel to remain in the target area for more than a few minutes. This was obviously not the case, as any student of Mirage and A-4 Skyhawk performance figures can easily establish. They had almost as much loiter time available over the target as did the Sea Harrier and, most importantly, they had the considerable advantage of being on the offensive and with vastly superior numbers. A further frequent comment has been that the attacking aircraft had no air-to-air weapons with which to fight. Having been on the receiving end of a Mirage's missile during the afternoon of 21 May, I can assure such detractors of the Sea Harrier's achievements that they have got it all wrong. Further, it is worthy of note that following 21 May (and with 1 May in mind) the Argentines christened Sea Harrier "The Black Death" (*La Muerte Negra*) and publicized this fact on their national radio broadcasts. They lived in fear of the Fleet Air Arm, though to their credit they continued with their almost suicidal offensive against our land and naval forces until Stanley fell.'

Ward and his No. 2, Lt. Steve Thomas, had a particularly good day on 21 May:

'We worked under the control of Lieutenant Commander Lea Hulme, who co-ordinated the Sea Harrier efforts against incoming raids from his operations room in HMS *Brilliant*. He gave tireless and invaluable service and established a strong rapport with my team. Through his information and comment we were able to begin to understand and appreciate the pressure being suffered by the ships in the Sound, and at the same time begin to understand that those ships' crews were literally fighting for their lives in a relatively indefensible stretch of water.

'The high morale and fighting spirit of our sailors was a tonic to us all, especially when *Brilliant*'s operations room was hit by cannon shells from Mirages: in spite of the mayhem all around, Lieutenant Commander Hulme never faltered, but kept his important commentary flowing.

'That commentary brought me my first kill when Steve Thomas, Lieutenant Commander Alistair Craig and I were vectored over the land near Goose Green to investigate a slow-moving contact. It turned out to be a Pucara which had been menacing our escorts in the Sound, and it did not take too long to destroy it with cannon fire. Nevertheless, the pilot stayed with it gallantly for as long as survival permitted and, having done everything possible to defend

Sea Harriers on the flight deck of HMS *Hermes*. A Sea King of the Carrier Air Group's rotary wing squadron is airlifting stores aboard.

A Sea Harrier launching
from the 850ft metal
runway at San Carlos.

himself, finally ejected just before his aircraft impacted the ground. I found out that his name was Major Tomba and that he was the leader of the "Toucan" Flight of Pucaras based at Goose Green. He was later to prove a most helpful interpreter for our medics during their treatment of the many Argentine casualties.'

Later in the day, Ward and Thomas were in action against three Daggers at low level over West Falkland. Thomas shot one of them down with a Sidewinder and launched his other AIM-9L at a second. The missile exploded close to the enemy aircraft. Thomas did not see it go down and so claimed only a 'probable'; in fact, the Dagger crashed. Meanwhile a third Dagger, closing head-on with Ward, fired an AAM – which missed – just before the two aircraft passed each other canopy to canopy. Ward pulled his Sea Harrier round hard, launched a Sidewinder and saw the Dagger go into the ground.

HMS *Invincible*'s complement of Sea Harriers had now been increased by four aircraft from the newly arrived No. 809 Squadron,

taking some of the strain off No. 801 following the earlier loss of two of its own aircraft. The main task remained CAP, although the Squadron carried out some ground attack sorties, including a night attack on Argentine positions on Pebble Island, using Lepus flares to illuminate the target area. In terms of air combat, however, it was No. 800 Squadron that got all the action during the next few days.

On 29 May, No. 801 Squadron suffered an accident that cost one Sea Harrier, fortunately without loss of life. Lt. Cdr. Mike Broadwater was preparing to take off in very bad weather when the carrier entered a tight turn and the aircraft slid over the wet deck to fall over the side. Broadwater ejected just as it went over and was rescued.

The first day of June provided Lt. Cdr. Ward of No. 801 Squadron with his third and final kill of the war. Together with Steve Thomas, he was climbing out from the San Carlos area en route to HMS *Invincible* when the frigate HMS *Minerva* reported a fleeting contact away to the north-west. The two Sea Harriers diverted to take a look, and Ward's radar screen imme-

diately showed a good, solid contact, heading west under low cloud. Descending through the cloud, Ward was elated to find a C-130 Hercules just a few miles ahead. Time was short because of Ward's fuel state, so he quickly fired both Sidewinders and all his 30mm ammunition into the enemy aircraft. The Hercules dropped its right wing and nose-dived, burning, into the sea.

Not long after this, No. 801 Squadron sustained another loss, this time due to enemy action, when Flt. Lt. Ian Mortimer, the Squadron air warfare instructor, was shot down in XZ456 by a Roland surface-to-air missile, about seven miles south of Port Stanley. Mortimer ejected successfully and was drifting in his dinghy close to the enemy-held shore, with night falling rapidly. His precise position was not known, and *Invincible* immediately mounted a full-scale helicopter search for him. The No. 820 Squadron command team of Ralph Wykes-Sneyd, Keith Dudley and Peter Galloway conducted a superb search and rescue operation which eventually culminated in Mortimer being snatched from under the enemy's noses after nine hours' survival in a freezing sea.

FALKLANDS GUARD DUTY

With the end of hostilities, Admiral Woodward detached *Invincible* for a period of self-maintenance, leaving *Hermes* to hold the air defence role for two weeks. *Invincible* returned to duty on 2 July, having become the first ship to change an engine (an Olympus gas turbine) while on active duty at sea. She was to remain while *Hermes* sailed home, so the latter detached two Sea Harriers to her to bring her complement up to strength.

To emphasize the strength and continued serviceability of the *Hermes* Air Group prior to the departure north, a massive flypast was made from the deck, over the ship and then over Stanley. It began with twelve helicopters and was followed by no fewer than sixteen Harriers – eleven Royal Navy Sea Harriers and five RAF Harrier GR.3s. The expertise gained through many weeks of operations with an average of seventeen Harriers on deck enabled all sixteen to be launched in five minutes, and recovered in just over seven.

On 4 July, the battle-scarred Harrier GR.3s of No. 1 Squadron disembarked to Stanley airfield and the *Hermes* sailed north for home. HMS *Invincible* remained as the principal Falklands

HMS *Hermes* comes home to Portsmouth in July 1982 bearing the scars inflicted upon her by the appalling operating conditions in the South Atlantic.

Invincible's triumphant homecoming, 17 September 1982.

A Sea Harrier of No. 801 Squadron leaving HMS *Invincible* after the carrier's homecoming on 17 September 1982.

guard ship until she was relieved, late in August, by HMS *Illustrious*, commissioned only two months earlier. With her, the carrier brought No. 809 Squadron, which kept two Sea Harriers permanently ashore at Stanley for the next two months, alongside the Harrier GR.3s of No. 1 Squadron, together with three pilots and eight ground crew. The squadron rotated the shore-based personnel every few days, to give everyone the chance to stretch their legs. While ashore, the personnel assisted in the routine air defence of the island, and, in addition, the RAF flew from *Illustrious* from time to time. At the end of the year, *Illustrious* and No. 809 Squadron came home, and on 17 December 1982 the squadron disbanded, its aircraft being dispersed among the other three Sea Harrier squadrons.

CONCLUSIONS

There are few who would even dare to dispute the fact that without the Sea Harrier and its RAF counterpart, the Harrier GR.3, the Falkland Islands would never have been re-taken. The Sea Harrier's excellent poor-weather capability paid for itself time after time in the Falklands; unlike the aircraft, the South Atlantic weather was extraordinarily unpredict-able and, occasionally, very bad, the biggest threats being fog and snowstorms. Most pilots launched in fog at least a couple of times, and on several occasions at night, and one pilot of No.

801 Squadron, Lt. C. Cantan, actually re-covered to the deck of the *Invincible* by night in fog, when the port deck-edge could not be seen from the bridge. Such versatility could not possibly be matched by any other naval aircraft.

Apart from its ability to operate in conditions that would have kept conventional fighter aircraft on the ground, the Sea Harrier and Harrier GR.3 withstood battle damage and proved simple to repair. However, the most striking outcome of the entire campaign, as far as the Sea Harrier was concerned, was the incredibly high serviceability provided by this small group of overworked aircraft, operating from just two carriers. Even during the early periods of the campaign, figures of 80–85 per cent availability were being reported; at the end of the conflict, initial government sources confirmed 85 per cent overall; and that figure later rose to an astonishing 95 per cent, as subsequently confirmed by the air engineering officers of the Sea Harrier squadrons in the two carriers.

There were, inevitably, Sea Harrier losses in the South Atlantic, but most of these were caused either by the appalling weather con-ditions or as a result of heavy ground fire during low-flying sorties in support of ground forces. The Harriers were never bettered in air-to-air combat by the supersonic aggressors pitted against them. The combination of the Sea Harrier and the AIM-9L Sidewinder AAM

Sea Harrier ZA176 in company with XZ438, the first development aircraft. The formation shows the contrasting colour schemes that resulted from operations in the South Atlantic.

HMS *Hermes* at Portsmouth following the Falklands War.

proved formidable, and one of the important decisions to emerge from the Falklands War was to equip the Royal Navy's Sea Harriers to carry four Sidewinders instead of two. The ordnance carried by the Sea Harrier also proved effective, although in air-to-air combat the Royal Navy pilots were seldom able to get close enough to Argentine aircraft to engage them with their cannon; in fact, only five Argentine aircraft were destroyed by the Sea Harrier's 30mm Adens, against eighteen destroyed by Sidewinders, and most of these were helicopters. Only one attacking Argentine jet aircraft, a Skyhawk, was shot down as a result of a cannon-only engagement. Had the Sea Harrier possessed a higher speed margin in combat, the result might have been

This post-Falklands photograph shows, nearest the camera, the first of the Hawker Hunter T.8 two-seaters specially modified to test the Sea Harrier's range of operational equipment. The Hunter is in formation with a Sea Harrier FRS.1 and a Harrier T.4N of No. 899 (Headquarters and Training) Squadron.

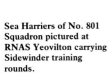

different, which argues the case for a transonic V/STOL Harrier development.

The experiences of the Falklands are still being evaluated today, but one of the early decisions taken by the British Government, after the cease-fire, was to order an additional fourteen Sea Harriers for the Royal Navy and also to announce the intention of replacing all the RAF Harrier GR.3s that were lost. In addition, it was proved conclusively that it is impractical to operate only two carriers within the fleet. This resulted in a stay of execution for the *Invincible*, which was, at one time, to be sold or leased to Australia, and although HMS *Hermes* has now been sold to India the Royal Navy still maintains a three-carrier force with *Invincible*, *Illustrious* and *Ark Royal*. It is now agreed that three carriers will continue in service, so guaranteeing that at least two ships will be in commission and available at any time.

Sea Harriers of No. 801
Squadron. Note the
chequered tail markings.

Periodically, the Royal Navy's Sea Harrier squadrons send detachments to the Air Combat Manoeuvring Instrumentation (ACMI) range at Decimomannu in Sardinia for realistic combat training. One of twelve such ranges throughout the world, Decimomannu is the only one in Europe. These facilities – the equivalent US Navy designation is Tactical Aircrew Combat Training System (TACTS) – provide fighter pilots with the opportunity for aggressive combat in realistic conditions without requiring special targets, live missiles or, more importantly, the possible loss of a pilot or aircraft.

One of the busiest ACMI ranges, Decimomannu – 'Deci' for short – became operational in 1979 for the training of NATO fast jet pilots. The United States and West Germany provide 35 per cent of the funding for its support, the United Kingdom 20 per cent and Italy 10 per cent. These figures are proportional to the amount of time each nation's air force uses the range.

The range is a 30nm diameter circle over the sea, about 50nm off the west coast of Sardinia, with a base height of 5,000ft and a ceiling of 50,000ft. Any aircraft straying from the circle, unless en route to or from the range, can be recalled to base by the local coastal radar at Mirto. This applies particularly to the adjacent north-west area outside the range where there is a civilian air route.

THE ACMI SYSTEMS

The ACMI consists of four principal linked elements, the Airborne Instrumentation Subsystem, the Tracking and Communication Subsystem, the Computer and Computation Subsystem and the Range Training Officer's Console. The Airborne Instrumentation Subsystem (AIS) is a pylon-attached transponder pod, with locking and connection points identical to those of the AIM-9 Sidewinder and linked to the aircraft's electrical, avionic and weapon systems. The AIS pod communicates directly with the Tracking and Communication Subsystem (TCS). This equipment is located in four 35-ton buoys moored at sea beneath the range,

one in the centre and the others around the circumference at 45°, 180° and 315°. Two additional unmanned land-based monitoring units located on mountains to the north and south of Decimomannu complete the remote part of the TCS. The information is passed from the remote units to the land-base manned TCS master station situated some 4,000ft up a mountain north of Decimomannu. The TCS master station feeds the information by microwave links to the Computer and Computation Subsystem (CCS) at Decimomannu. The CCS processes the data received from each aircraft – altitude, speed, bearing, angle of attack and what types of missile are programmed into it – and if a missile is launched it calculates the range and simulated track of the weapon in relation to the dynamic track of its selected target.

From the CCS computers, the data is passed to two 6ft square graphical VDU screen displays above the Range Training Officer's console and can be viewed by an audience of up to about twenty. It is the responsibility of the RTOs to monitor the exercise, vector their pilots to the opposition, saving range time and simulating ground radar control, and have radio contact with their own pilots. Not only can the audience see the aircraft in plan view, but the image can be rotated through 90° to give an elevation. Further, a second screen, which is normally utilized for an alphanumeric display of the aircraft data, can be used to show a graphical cockpit view of any selected combatant. When an aircraft is 'killed', a 'coffin' shape appears round it and the pilot is vectored out of the fight by his RTO for 45 seconds, at which point he is free to return and the 'coffin' is removed. During this period, the computer will not recognize, nor therefore record, any missile launch or gun firing from the 'killed' aircraft.

The length of combat time over the range is strictly controlled to 20-minute slots for the aircraft using the facility. At the end of their slot the pilots return and debrief using a video recording of the combat at the Display and Debrief Subsystem (DDS). They can view this recording, freezing a frame or using play-back

A Sea Harrier of No. 800 Squadron intercepts a Soviet Tu-95 'Bear' maritime reconnaissance aircraft in the course of a NATO exercise.

Rocket-firing practice by a Sea Harrier of No. 800 Squadron.

to identify mistakes, lost opportunities and incidents during the range slot and get a clear and complete overall picture of the recently concluded combat.

WAR GAMES

A detachment of No. 899 Headquarters and Training Squadron went to Decimomannu in June 1984, and this particular detachment serves to illustrate what happens at the range. The purpose of the exercise was a continuation of the training of student Sea Harrier pilots and the investigation of new tactics. The detachment, with a total of about 80 personnel, was led by the Commanding Officer, Lt. Cdr. Denis Thornton, and included four Sea Harriers and two T.8M Hunters. The principal task of the detachment was to provide air combat experience for two student pilots, Lt. Ted O'Connell and Lt. Tim Mannion, and priority was given to their sorties over all others. The detailed debriefing facilities were of particular value to them in their role as trainees.

During the early stages of No. 899's detachment, some minor difficulties were experienced with the aircraft's electrical equipment and the engines, which required some adjustments to compensate for a different fuel being used.

Fortunately, No. 899 had included Mr. Martin Webb, the Yeovilton-base Rolls-Royce representative, who was quickly put to work to assist the ground crew tuning the engines and the Squadron 'Greenies' sorting out the electrical problems.

During the first week, No. 899 acquired a back-up RTO in the form of Capt. Dave Kuhn USAF, from the 602nd Tactical Squadron, based in Turkheim, West Germany. He soon received the nickname of 'Zorro'. 'Zorro' assisted No. 899's own RTO and Direction Officer (the 'D'), Lt. Tim Kelly, working alternate sorties, attending the briefings, taking charge of the Cubic control cabin during the combat and then running through the debrief with the pilots.

At the end of the first week, Lt. Cdr. Thornton was content with the progress of the student training programme and opened negotiations with the USAF for a sortie against F-5s and F-15s in a two-versus-two-versus-two, although, as one would expect, it ended up as a two-plus-two-versus-two. In this first sortie against foreign nationals were two Sea Harriers (SHARS), flown by Lt. Cdr. Thornton and Lt. Dave Morgan with the call-signs 'Bentley 1' and 'Bentley 2' respectively. The F-5s were provided by the 527th Tactical Fighter Training

Sea Harriers of No. 899 Headquarters and Training Squadron pictured at the NATO Air Combat Manoeuvring Instrumentation Range at Decimomannu in Sardinia (top). One of the busiest ACMI Ranges, Decimomannu became operational in 1979 for the training of NATO fast jet pilots.

The flight line at Decimomannu (above). In this photograph, Jaguars of the Royal Air Force rub shoulders with F-15s and F-5 Aggressors of USAFE.

One of 899's Sea Harriers at Decimomannu.

Aggressor Squadron based at Alconbury, and the F-15s from the 32nd Tactical Fighter Squadron based in Germany.

The 20-minute sorties showed the vast difference between American and British tactics and roles. Both US types remained at high level in the initial stages, where their greater performance could be used to effect, the F-5s loitering at 35,000ft while the F-15 Eagles held themselves aloof at 40,000ft watching the fight developing

beneath them. At first the SHARS were opposed by the F-5s only, but within minutes of engagement, the latter were beginning to run out of fuel owing to the fact that they were not fitted with drop tanks and because of the necessity for them to use afterburners almost constantly. With the F-5s out of the fight, the stage was clear for the SHARS to tackle the F-15s. Combat was still at high level, though one of the F-15s tended to get much lower than its

A Sidewinder training round under the starboard wing of a Sea Harrier at Decimomannu.

partner and 'mix it'. Unsupported by his consort, the result was almost a foregone conclusion. He was hit repeatedly, whilst on one occasion his wingman actually departed from the confines of the range – leaving his leader alone.

The debriefing between the six pilots was equally interesting in that the techniques and intentions adopted by the pairs now came to light. The F-5 approach was to remain at medium to high level to draw the SHARS up to them, while the Eagles chose the high position, swooping down occasionally to pick off a target before returning to high level to repeat the tactics. The SHARS, on the other hand, attempted to draw the opposition down to low/medium level. In analysis, no one got what they wanted, but it was a good compromise and laid a strong foundation for future combined sorties. Lt. Cdr. Thornton was clearly disappointed by the result (as far as hits were concerned the scoring was equal) and he wanted improvement. By the same token, his USAF counterpart also expressed the same reaction and both departed for the weekend with food for thought.

The second Monday of the detachment brought with it a repeat of Friday's two-versus-two-versus-two sortie with the USAF squad-

An Airborne Instrumentation Subsystem transponder pod attached to the port wing of a Sea Harrier at Decimomannu.

rons. Each had indeed learned from Friday's combat and they reversed their previous tactics. This time the Eagles came in at about 7,000ft while the SHARS were up at 20,000ft and the F-5s again about half-way between the two formations. The SHARS, flown by Sq. Ldr. Matheson, senior pilot, and Lt. Cdr. Watson, managed to stay together as a pair for the bulk of the time, repeatedly proving the effectiveness of a pair working in unison and having a high score to show for it.

Later that morning another joint exercise took

One of a new batch of Sea Harriers is collected by 'Soapy' Watson of 899 Squadron from the British Aerospace field at Dunsfold.

A pair of Sea Harriers of No. 899 Squadron over the rolling landscape of south-west England. Note that the nearer aircraft is carrying four Sidewinders in twin launchers, an arrangement cleared for operational use after the Falklands War.

place, this time with a pair of SHARS versus a pair of F-15s. Unfortunately one of the F-15s went unserviceable prior to take-off, but his partner carried on alone. On this sortie there was a requirement to prove the intercept geometry required for a side-on shot against a supersonic target. The lone F-15, flown by Capt. Davies, consequently went to the north of the range, turned and increased speed until he had reached Mach 1.19 at an altitude of 26,000ft, and was heading for the SHAR pair. Lt. Hargreaves and Lt. Morgan took on this interception, and as the F-15 closed with them they turned in to fire and brought the engagement to a successful conclusion.

When the SHARS returned to Decimomannu in close formation with the Eagles, the sheer size of the US aircraft was apparent. In fact the F-15 pilots admitted to having considerable difficulty in picking out the Harrier due to its size. To quote one of them, 'I was up at 35,000ft and when I looked down I had great trouble seeing you guys. When I did, you looked like a couple of bugs'. True – but bugs that would bite back, as they found out.

The Thursday of that second week also saw a solo SHAR demonstration at the base by Lt. Morgan – the only demonstration by any aircraft during the fortnight – and later that same day the first sortie was flown against West German Air Force F-4s. Four F-14 Tomcats from the nuclear-powered attack carrier USS *Saratoga* also arrived. As might be expected, the *Luftwaffe* proved to be very competent and professional in their approach, the tactics involving a pincer attack manoeuvre which proved very effective. The first sortie was very disappointing for No. 899 Squadron, but the second showed great improvement with the SHARS splitting up the F-4s before picking them off one by one. The Germans tended to enter combat flying parallel but with one aircraft 2,000–3,000ft higher than its consort. Allowing the SHARS to pass between them, the F-4s would turn inwards simultaneously, giving them a choice of target to pick off. However, the SHARS managed to keep them apart during subsequent sorties and outmanoeuvre them, preventing them from acting as a pair. Unfortunately the last sortie of No. 899 Squadron's detachment to Decimomannu, again versus F-4s, was cancelled because of the closure of the field as a result of the loss of an Italian Air Force Starfighter.

No. 899 Squadron's detachment to the Decimomannu range in Sardinia proved to be an unqualified success. From the early days of the fortnight, when the unit had consisted of

A Sea Harrier of No. 899 Squadron venting fuel.

Sea Harriers of Nos. 899 and 800 Squadrons show their paces at Farnborough in September 1982. Note the different shades of grey in the aircraft's colour schemes.

individual experts in their own fields of instruction, each primarily concerned with his own responsibilities, the unit had been drawn together to form a very close-knit community and providing each other with maximum support. This was particularly apparent during the dissimilar combat sorties against the F-5s, F-15s and F-4s – more so than during inter-unit combats, when pilots know each other as personalities and are familiar with the opposing aircraft and current thinking on tactics. Against unfamiliar pilots and aircraft, however, the situation changed radically, and lengthy discussions took place on tactics and aircraft capabilities, both inside and outside briefing and debriefing rooms, often well into the night.

Like any NATO squadron that uses Deci-momannu, No. 899 went away a much sharper and more capable unit than when it first arrived. The two least experienced pilots, Lts.

A Sea Harrier of No. 899 Squadron on the flight line at RNAS Yeovilton.

O'Connell and Mannion, in particular had found it an invaluable experience to see the fight from their attacker's point of view on the RTO's display screens, assessing any mistakes they themselves had made through their opponent's eyes. Like others using the ACMI system, they had learned in a fortnight what it used to take junior pilots several months to learn – and, as the pilots of both the Royal Navy and Royal Air Force found when they were pitched into the Falklands War in May 1982, the time available for an operational squadron to prepare for action might be measured in days rather than weeks.

A Sea Harrier of No. 801 Naval Air Squadron plugs into a US Navy KA-6 Intruder tanker during Exercise 'Caribtrain' in 1983. (Crown Copyright)

India's involvement with the Sea Harrier began in July 1972 when John Farley, then Deputy Chief Test Pilot of Hawker Siddeley Aviation at Kingston, carried out a series of trials aboard the Indian aircraft carrier INS *Vikrant* (formerly the British *Majestic* Class light fleet carrier HMS *Hercules*) using the two-seat Harrier Mk. 52 demonstrator, registered G-VTOL by the Department of Trade and Industry.

The uneventful ferry flight to India was routed from Dunsfold via Naples, Akrotiri, Tehran, Kuwait, Masirah and Bombay to Cochin, the Indian Navy base on the south-west tip of the sub-continent. The ground crew followed along each leg in a Hawker Siddeley 748. The flight plans having been laid two months earlier, the Harrier arrived at Bombay only twenty minutes late, but monsoon conditions delayed the aircraft's arrival at Cochin by a day, which meant that the two days allowed for work-up flying from the airfield, prior to em-

barking on *Vikrant*, had to be shrunk into a single day – which caused some problems for Capt. R. H. Tahiliani, the Director, Air Staff Division, Indian Navy, who was to fly in the rear seat.

DEMONSTRATION EXERCISE

Since the captain had not previously flown the Harrier, he had to train very intensively to reach the standard necessary for him to control the aircraft in the confined environment of the deck. Nevertheless, Tahiliani was a highly experienced naval aviator (he had been the first Indian Navy officer to land a Hawker Sea Hawk on board *Vikrant*), and he responded well to the challenge. It was agreed that Farley would fly the aircraft solo on the first day and that Capt. Tahiliani and two other officers would join in on the second day.

G-VTOL, which had been the first two-seat Harrier to fly with the Pegasus 102 engine, was

A Sea Harrier FRS Mk. 51, in the livery of the Indian Navy, is demonstrated at Farnborough.

now equipped with the updated Pegasus 103 of 21,500lb thrust, in order to be cleared for world-wide demonstration work. The aircraft was also equipped with a larger range of radio/navigation aids (such as INS and ADF) than the standard RAF two-seaters, making the aircraft longer and some 1,500lb heavier. As the aircraft had never been flown from a ship in this configur-ation, Farley and Robbie Roberts, the Hawker Siddeley Aviation, Kingston, Sales Executive, were at pains to point out to the Indian Navy that they only had estimates of the performance that was likely to be achieved by the aircraft during trials on the *Vikrant*. Moreover, initial trials would require cautious test flying rather than a simple sales demonstration, allowing them to establish the weight that could be lifted from various deck runs in the hot monsoon conditions expected off the Indian coast in July.

Getting G-VTOL on to *Vikrant* was not easy, although the weather was not too bad: there was no cloud but, at low level, the visibility was decidedly murky – about a mile in a humid sub-tropical haze over the sea. Farley later admitted that he was very nervous; nevertheless, his accrued skills enabled him to bring the aircraft down to a safe landing on the carrier's flight deck.

Once on board, a meeting was held with the ship's officers and all the engineering, adminstrative and flying control aspects were quickly dealt with. All that remained was to decide what markings would be painted on the deck. In the end, Farley settled for a 2ft wide centreline down the axial length of the deck, a white line across the bows of the ship for the 'nozzles down' indication and a broken line down the starboard side of the deck, parallel with the centreline, for use as a 'wing tip safety line' and behind which all other parked aircraft, men and equipment would be positioned while a short take-off was in progress.

The deck markings were painted just where Farley had wanted them, but, unfortunately, the 2ft wide centreline, down which the Harrier would run, was painted in high-gloss paint which was very slippery indeed when it was wet: since the Harrier was controlled directionally by nosewheel steering, it was clear to Farley that he would have to run slightly to one side of the line. This caused some concern at first, as the obstacle clearance to the left-hand side, with the Harrier on the line, was only 8½ft, and running to the right of the line would have taken the wingtip uncomfortably close to the parked

aircraft. However, there was an additional line already painted on the deck, 7ft to the left of the Harrier line and parallel to it, so it appeared that, provided the Harrier operated between these two lines, all would be well.

After a short period of taxying around the deck to familiarize the deck handlers with the Harrier, Farley was all set for the first take-off. This was done at a light weight, down the full length of the 660ft axial deck. The technique went well and was retained, in principle, throughout the two days' flying. It consisted of free-taxying the Harrier into position at the start of the run, running up to 55 per cent rpm, with the brakes on and the nozzles almost aft at 8° down from the horizontal. Then, on being given clearance to take off, the brakes were released, full throttle was applied, and the left hand was moved from the throttle to the nozzle lever as the run began. The aircraft was steered with the nosewheel, controlled by the rudder pedals, and then finally, when the white line across the end of the deck reached the bottom of the wind-screen, the nozzles were lowered to the desired angle marked by a pre-set stop. Although the first sortie from *Vikrant* presented no problems, a second sortie was made at the same light weight to allow Farley to feel certain that he was used to the technique. Afterwards, the all-up weight was progressively increased by the input of more fuel.

The third take-off was done with full internal fuel, and the fourth through to the eighth were all at full internal fuel, although the distance of the starting point from the front end of the deck was reduced to as little as 370ft. For the remain-ing take-offs on the first day, the Harrier was made as heavy as possible using fuel alone, with the 100 Imp. gallon combat drop tanks full, and the run was eventually reduced, at this maximum weight, to 585ft. After the eleventh flight, the aircraft was landed back at Cochin for the night.

The first six flights on the second day were made with Captain Tahiliani flying in the rear of the cockpit. Despite his inexperience in the aeroplane and the fact that he was currently employed in a senior staff post and not on full-time flying duty, the Indian officer had no difficulty in taking control of the Harrier outside the hangar at Cochin, and flying entirely un-aided into a hover astern of *Vikrant* 20 minutes later. By the end of his six flights, Tahiliani had flown a take-off himself on the full length of the axial deck and had accompanied Farley on the first angled deck take-off using the short (317ft) angled deck run. In addition, Farley demonstrated a cross-deck vertical landing, just aft of the island, to show the technique used when recovering a Harrier if the ship is not steaming into wind. Captain Tahiliani then gave up his seat to Cdr. Grewal, the Commander (Air) of *Vikrant*.

Grewal, being a current Sea Hawk and helicopter pilot, found himself delighted with the Harrier and he carried out a decelerating transition to a hover alongside the ship, followed by an accelerating transition back to wingborne flight with no assistance from Farley other than the odd word of encouragement. The three remaining flights that day were with Cdr. Raju, a Sea Hawk squadron commander, in the second seat and included a vertical take-off from the bow of the ship and a heavyweight, 310ft, deck-run short take-off.

The exercise finished as planned at the end of the second day. The two days with *Vikrant* had resulted in 21 Harrier sorties at an ambient temperature of 30°C (86°F).

FIRST EXPORT PROGRAMME

The successful demonstration by Farley to the Indian Navy of the Harrier's obvious advantages in naval operations led, in 1980, to an Indian Government order for six Sea Harrier FRS.51s and two two-seat Harrier T.60s, for delivery in 1983. The Sea Harriers were to be operated by No. 300 (White Tiger) Squadron, at that time the Indian Navy's Sea Hawk unit. In the meantime, INS *Vikrant* underwent a refit, during which she was equipped with a ski-ramp. Arrangements were made for the posting of Indian Navy pilots and engineers to the United Kingdom for V/STOL conversion and engineering/maintenance training. The first small group of Indian Navy personnel arrived in the UK to commence their training in October 1982; more groups followed, the main party arriving in December that year.

December 1982 also saw the maiden flight of the first Indian FRS.51, the first export Sea Harrier. It was formally handed over to the Indian Navy by the Kingston-Brough Division of British Aerospace in January 1983. After the

Sea Harrier FRS.51s of No. 300 'White Tiger' Squadron pose for the camera before their delivery flight to India.

The handover of the first Sea Harrier FRS.51 to the Indian Navy, January 1983.

aircraft was accepted by the Indian High Commissioner in London, Dr. Seyid Muhamed, a Vedic ritual of Muhurtha was carried out by the High Commissioner's wife, together with Mrs. Seetha Gupta, the wife of the Indian Naval Adviser in London. In the brief ceremony, the two ladies took a silver platter, or *thali*, bearing a ritual flame and incense, to the aircraft, and a garland of marigolds was draped over the Sea Harrier's pitot tube, followed by a smear of vermillion paste on the nose cone. The final part of the ceremony consisted of a coconut being smashed on the floor, near the Sea Harrier's nosewheel, to bring success to all those who would fly it. By February 1983, the Indian Navy complement at RNAS Yeovilton had grown to over one hundred personnel and two aircraft; the total number of Indian personnel to be trained would eventually comprise about 180 officers and men.

For the small group of Indian Navy pilots, all of whom had originally been flying Sea Hawks, training began under the auspices of No. 233 Operational Conversion Unit at RAF Wittering, where their initial V/STOL conversion was carried out. Having mastered the flying of V/STOL aircraft in the three-month conversion course, the first two groups of Indian Navy pilots moved to RNAS Yeovilton, where they converted to the Sea Harrier and were taught to use the aircraft as a weapons system, learning many of the tactics and techniques employed by the Royal Navy's Sea Harrier units. At Yeovilton, they joined No. 899 Headquarters and Training Squadron, where many of the instructors were able to pass on their considerable experience and knowledge, some of it gained during the Falklands conflict. Altogether, the Indian pilots spent about a year at Yeovilton, during which time they practised weapons delivery and air-to-air combat. They also used the training ramp at RNAS Yeovilton, and had the opportunity of carrying out ski-jump launches at sea from the 12° ramp of HMS *Hermes* when the carrier was available.

The first three Sea Harrier FRS.51s of No. 300 Indian Naval Air Squadron were delivered to their new base at Goa in December 1983 after a ferry flight of 4,800 nautical miles from the United Kingdom; the total flying time was 10 hours 13 minutes. Led by British Aerospace Test Pilot Lt. Cdr. Taylor Scott RNR, the formation left Yeovilton on 13 December 1983 for the first leg of the journey to Luqa airport, Malta, where they remained overnight and were turned round for the next day's sector. From Malta, with Cdr. Arun Prakash (No. 300 Squadron's CO) and Lt. Cdr. Sanjoy Gupta in

Nos. 2 and 3 positions, the formation flew on via Egypt to Dubai, the second overnight stop. The third and final sector was the longest part of the delivery, taking the aircraft direct to India, and Goa Naval Base, where work on the facilities for the new Sea Harrier-equipped squadron was then approaching completion. The remaining aircraft were delivered in the first quarter of 1984, when the flying and maintenance training of the last groups of Indian Navy personnel had been completed. No. 300 Squadron was fully operational on its new aircraft by the end of 1984.

In May 1986, the Indian Government ordered a second batch of Sea Harriers, a mixture of FRS.51s and T.60s, to form part of an expanding naval strike force that will operate from the former HMS *Hermes*; purchased by India, the carrier, renamed INS *Viraat*, is to be commissioned into the Indian Navy after re-fitting. The Indian Government has also taken out an option on a third contract involving an undisclosed number of Sea Harriers.

CONCLUSIONS

The likely operation of the Indian Navy's Sea Harriers must be viewed against the background of the country's continued tension with Pakistan. During the Indo-Pakistan War of December 1971, the carrier *Vikrant* launched a series of strikes with Sea Hawk aircraft against targets in what was then East Pakistan, notably Cox's Bazaar and Chittagong, causing severe damage to oil storage tanks, the dock areas and runway installations, and these operations undoubtedly helped the Indian army to secure a speedy victory in that area. In any future conflict, the Indian Navy's sphere of operations would almost certainly be the Arabian Sea, from which its carriers would be well placed to strike at important strategic targets in Pakistan itself. Such operations would not be without their attendant risks, for the Pakistan Air Force's Mirage III aircraft have sufficient range to strike at any Indian naval task force operating in that area. However, the Sea Harrier has given the Indian Navy an entirely new CAP capability which should provide an insurance against any surprise attack by Pakistan. With the latter increasingly embroiled in the fighting in Afghanistan, at least in the border area, the prospect of a new Indo-Pakistan conflict seems unlikely, and yet skirmishing still flares up from time to time along the disputed North-West Frontier border between the two countries. It is certain that the Indians do not intend to be caught unawares.

As a result of their experience with the AV-8A, the US Marine Corps decided that a V/STOL successor with improved performance, together with the high-performance F/A-18 attack fighter, would satisfy virtually all their air arm's requirements. The result was the AV-8B Harrier II.

The AV-8B owes its origins, in part, to the failure in 1974 of the joint UK/US V/STOL programme to produce an aircraft, the AV-16, powered by a 24,500lb thrust Pegasus 15 vectored thrust engine. The projected development cost, reportedly in excess of $US 1 billion, led to the programme's downfall. However, in a further collaborative programme, BAe and McDonnell Douglas were able to show the US Marine Corps that, with a number of airframe changes, the payload radius of the AV-8A could be greatly increased without the need to develop the engine. This was an attractive proposition to the USMC since, with the AV-8A, they had traded performance for effectiveness to acquire V/STOL flexibility.

STATE-OF-THE-ART HARRIER

The Harrier used 1950s technology in airframe design and construction and in systems, and by the 1970s, despite systems updates, this was restricting the further development of the aircraft's potential. In developing the USMC's new Harrier variant, the basic design concept was retained, but the new technologies and avionics were fully exploited. This demonstrates again, in the strongest of fashions, the capabilities of the Harrier's inherent, basic characteristics to be developed to meet the new and evolving demands of warfare – one of the fundamental tests of a truly successful weapons system.

One of the major improvements was a new wing, with a carbon fibre composite structure, a supercritical aerofoil and a greater area and span. The wing has large slotted flaps linked with nozzle deflection at STO unstick to improve control precision and increase lift. Leading-edge root extensions (LERX) are fitted to enhance the aircraft's air combat agility by improving the turn rate, while longitudinal fences (LIDS, or lift improvement devices) are incorporated beneath the fuselage and on the gun pods to capture ground-reflected jets in VTOL, give a much bigger ground cushion and reduce hot gas re-circulation. The wing contains 2,000lb more internal fuel than that of the AV-8A, and it is fitted with six hardpoints compared to the AV-8A's four. The forward fuselage is also partly manufactured in carbon-epoxy composite. The cockpit is positioned higher than the AV-8A's to provide additional space for avionics and, further enhanced by a new bubble canopy, to improve the pilot's view. The systems are considerable improvements over

One of the development AV-8B Harrier IIs, 161397.

USMC AV-8Bs demonstrate a short take-off from a forest road.

those of the Harrier/AV-8A, as the quoted passages on the following pages will make clear.

Powered by the Pegasus 11 (Mk. 105), the AV-8B – without an increase in engine thrust over the AV-8A – has double the AV-8A's payload/radius capability: armed with six Mk. 82 500lb bombs, for example, the AV-8B has a radius 55 per cent greater than that of the A-4M Skyhawk, and would use only 1,200ft of runway compared to the A-4M's 4,200ft. The Harrier II's maximum external payload of 9,200lb includes a wide range of conventional bombs, rockets, laser-guided weapons and air-to-air and air-to-surface missiles, as well as four 300 US gallon drop tanks.

Col. Harry Blot, USMC programme manager for the AV-8B, had this to say at the outset of the project:

'The AV-8A served its purpose, but the Harrier II will be more effective and so will the average pilot. It took a superior pilot to be effective in the A. The AV-8B is a simpler airplane to fly. It has more sophisticated systems to be able to survive in a high threat environment. It has better navigational equipment and considerably more accurate weapons delivery.'

It is this improved cockpit working environment that, from the pilot's viewpoint, is the

quintessential difference between the Harrier II
and the earlier AV-8A. Col. Blot continued:

'In the earlier AV-8A we had 1960s switch-
ology. In combat we found that, across the
board, what was acceptable in peacetime was no
longer acceptable in wartime. You are trying to
fight another airplane and you have a lot of 'g' on
you. In the AV-8A you must look and reach to
throw a switch, then turn around again. You
just can't do that when someone is trying to kill
you. You dont't want to take your eyes off him.

'Now in the AV-8B we have a system that will
allow you, without letting go of either throttle or
stick, to switch from an offensive to a defensive
mode and back again without ever taking your
eyes away from the enemy. So, if I'm running in
on target to destroy it and I'm being attacked,
then with one flick of the thumb the Harrier II
system changes all my sensors, arms my air-to-
air weapons, changes my displays, head up and
head down, and I am totally prepared for air
combat. If the attacker doesn't turn in, then one
more flick of my thumb and the aircraft goes
back to being optimized for air-to-ground. In
wartime that's absolutely vital.'

PROGRAMME BUILD-UP
Having received the go-ahead to proceed with
the development of an Advanced Harrier in
March 1976, McDonnell Douglas flew the first
of two YAV-8B aerodynamic prototypes,
converted from AV-8As, in November 1978.
The YAV-8Bs met or exceeded the predicted
performance, and in 1979 four full-scale
development AV-8Bs were ordered by the
USMC. Hawker Siddeley, soon to become part
of British Aerospace, agreed to build the centre
and rear fuselage sections and fins for these
aircraft.

The first development AV-8B (BuNo 161396)
flew on 26 February 1981. This was followed
later that year by a joint manufacturing agreement between McDonnell Douglas and British
Aerospace, calling for 328 AV-8Bs for the
USMC and 62 Harrier GR.5s for the Royal Air
Force. The four development AV-8Bs entered
their flight test programme in 1982, along with
the YAV-8B prototype, and the first production
AV-8B was handed over to Training Squadron
VMAT-203 at Cherry Point, North Carolina, on
16 January 1984, the aircraft making its
acceptance check flight four days later. Eleven
more AV-8Bs were delivered before the end of
1984, followed by another 21 in 1985.

By the summer of 1986, more than 60 AV-8Bs
had been delivered to Marine Aircraft Group
(MAG) 32, with deliveries from the St. Louis
factory of McDonnell Douglas continuing at the
rate of two or three per month. The one
hundredth AV-8B was handed over to the
USMC on 28 December 1987, completing the
equipment of five operational squadrons and
one training squadron. A sixth AV-8B squadron
was expected to form at MCAS Yuma in early
1989. MAG-32's sister-group is MAG-13, at El
Toro, California. Each Marine Aircraft Group
comprises four AV-8B tactical squadrons, each
with complements of 20 aircraft and 30 pilots.

TRAINING AND IOC
VMAT-203 began training pilots exclusively for
the AV-8B in the spring of 1985, and 170 had
completed their conversion course by the end of
1986. The advent of the AV-8B has seen a
considerable expansion of the USMC's training
syllabus: whereas VMAT-203 was training
about fifteen new pilots per year to fly the AV-
8A (making a total of about 300 since the earlier
Harrier type went into service in the early
1970s), up to 90 student pilots graduate on the
AV-8B each year. To cope with this increase,
VMAT-203's strength has been expanded to 45
instructors and an aircraft complement of 30
single- and two-seat AV-8B/TAV-8Bs.

Pilots converting to the AV-8B with VMAT-
203 arrive at Cherry Point through three
channels. The first of these is provided by
former AV-8A pilots who undergo a week of
ground school, a week of simulated training,
and then between 14 and 17 hours of AV-8B
flying before assignment to a tactical squadron
with which, after a further three months, they
are considered operational. Pilots passing
through the second channel have come from the
A-4M Skyhawk, and fly fifteen sorties in the
TAV-8A before going solo in the AV-8B. They
can fly some 50 sorties before being assigned to a
squadron. The third channel is Naval Air
Training Command (NATC), for which pilots
arrive direct for conversion, these also flying
fifteen TAV-8A sorties and then up to 65 AV-8B
sorties.

According to Lt. Col. John W. Capito,
former Commanding Officer of VMAT-203, the
training process has been radically simplified by
comparison with that for the earlier AV-8A.
This, he says, is due to a combination of
excellent flying characteristics on the part of the
AV-8B, with its three-axis stability augmen-

tation and attitude-hold system significantly reducing pilot workload in V/STOL operation, and the use of realistic simulators.

AV-8B training has led to an enormous increase in the simulator training facility at Cherry Point, which now possesses an operational flight trainer and a weapons tactics trainer. The flight trainer provides realistic, computer-generated imagery depicting terrain, various landing sites (including locations used for austere site training in the Lynam Road Exercise Area at the nearby Camp Lejeune) and such amphibious assault vessels as the USS *Guam* and *Tarawa*. The weapons tactics trainer enables pilots to utilize the full capabilities of the AV-8B's weapons system and ECM equipment while opposed by simulated sophisticated enemy defences.

The first of MAG-32's tactical squadrons to convert to the AV-8B was VMA-331, the 'Bumblebees', which achieved IOC with an initial batch of twelve aircraft early in 1985. The Squadron's strength had risen to fifteen in the autumn of 1986 and had reached the full complement of 20 by March 1987. The second AV-8B tactical squadron, VMA-231, achieved

Harrier IIs of VMA-331

An AV-8B carrying sixteen 570lb Mk. 82 bombs.

A VMA-331 AV-8B releasing a pair of retarded bombs over a desert practice range.

IOC in July 1986 with fifteen aircraft, and a third squadron, VMA-457, also achieved IOC at the end of 1986. The fourth squadron to convert was the first of the West Coast units, VMA-513, based at Yuma, which had stood down as the last of the Marine Corps' AV-8A squadrons in August 1986.

FLYING HARRIER II

The opinion of the US Marine Corps' pilots on the AV-8B is reflected in the words of two men who were heavily involved in its introduction into service, Lt. Col. Mike Nyalko, who was an

AV-8B test pilot at Patuxent River in 1985, and Lt. Col. Jimmy Cranford, who, as the Commanding Officer of VMA-331 at Cherry Point, helped to introduce the AV-8B into service at the same time. Nyalko was highly complimentary about the AV-8B's departure resistant system (DRS) which feeds the stability augmentation system and ensures carefree handling. Nyalko commented:

'It's an excellent system. I had it up to 122 degrees angle of attack [AoA], that's in a vertical axis viffing [thrust vectoring in forward flight]

A photograph of a 'clean' AV-8B, clearly showing the underwing stores stations.

maneuver, called a flop. You select 30 degrees nozzle and augment it with full back stick, which gives you about 40 degrees/second pitch like an extremely tight loop. The airplane seems to revolve around its axis when seen from outside, and we use it to change from nose up to nose down in combat.

'I know 122 degrees sounds strange, but the airplane keeps going in the same direction as when you start it. In more conventional [wingborne] flight, and compared with the AV-8A, we can pull 30 alpha [degrees of AoA] at slow speeds compared with the A's 18 alpha, and at M 0.8 we can do 20 alpha. Get the CG aft, and you can pull all the alphas you want. On instantaneous turn rate we're about a third up on the A. Sustained turn rate is about the same because the thrust-to-drag ratio is about the same on the B as the A. We've more power on the B, but also a little more drag.

'Going on the boat or into a confined site, the B is a drastic improvement over the A. Control of the aircraft is not your prime consideration any more, like it was in the A. Your field of view is much better and you occasionally look inside to monitor the engine, but you can spend much more time looking at the boat or wherever. In the A, I was always worried about the engine performance, thrust and all that. Also, in the B

the stability is better. We don't use attitude hold.

'Another nice thing is OBOGS [on-board oxygen generating system]. That's the biggest system advance I've seen since I started flying. The system is very reliable – one failure in 2,000 hours and that was on Day Three. In the AV-8A, when we did trans-Pacific deployments, we were limited by the oxygen we had, not fuel or oil. With OBOGS you could stay up as long as there are tankers. Another OBOGS plus is that our amphibious ships have no liquid-oxygen manufacturing capability, so we had to bring oxygen carts by helicopter from a CV [fleet carrier] or carry a bunch of it on the ship; the same when we deployed ashore. Now, no problem, no liquid-oxygen handling problems, and quicker, safer turnarounds.

'The ARBS [Angle Rate Bombing System] is also extremely impressive. That thing makes the AV-8B the most accurate air-to-ground platform the US Navy has ever developed. I figure dispersion of weapons will be a problem, really. I've dropped all the 50s and 80s series bombs except the 2,000lb Mk. 84, because that's got 30in lug spacing and we have 14in pylons. Most on one hop? Sixteen Mk. 82s on triple ejector racks, personally.

'The RAF guys are really going to be im-

An underside view of an AV-8B, showing a clutch of retarded bombs and the underfuselage cannon.

pressed with this aeroplane. It's more accurate as a weapon delivery platform than the Harrier, it is much easier to get to the target with, its combat capability is a big improvement, it manoeuvres better, it goes further, and it won't depart on you. With that DRS you can pull as hard as you like at any airspeed and the airplane will just turn. You can feed in some really gross control inputs and it won't depart on you. I don't think honestly that any of the squadron pilots will ever go out as far as it's been on test, Marines or RAF – I don't think they'll find a limit.'

However, there were things about the AV-8B that Mike Nyalko did not like:

'That's the beauty of this job. If we don't like it, they change it. That's what we're here for. But, yes, there have been things and we've changed them. For instance, the master warning panel was down behind my right knee. You only get an aural warning for red-light warnings, so you could fly along with a cluster of amber caution lights behind your knee and not know it. So we changed that and have an up-front advisory light now, near the HUD. That was part of the problem with this airplane, you're heads-up most times anyway.

'I also want a moving map display like the RAF will have. The INS we have is very good, but gives read-outs as Universal Transverse Mercator grid coordinates, down to 100-meter squares. But there's no way to update that in

flight, and UTM grids don't tell me where mountains are, so I carry a map. We really need that moving map for the Marine mission and it'll be available in 1988 for the night-attack AV-8B, so we ought to get it now.'

At Cherry Point, VMA-331's Commanding Officer, Lt. Col. Cranford, is an old VTOL hand, having joined the 'Harrier Mafia' at RAF Wittering in 1972 after flying 132 A-4 Skyhawk missions over Vietnam with VMA-311 at Chu Lai Air Base. Cranford is an unabashed AV-8B fan:

'It's a hell of a good aircraft. When we got the first one, we flew the pants off it, and it did 70 hours in its first month. Now we've pulled back the reins a bit and we're looking at about 40 hours per month for each aircraft, and running maybe sixteen sorties a day with the six total I have right now. The life at present is 6,000 hours, so if we continued at the initial rate – well, the Corps would need to buy us some more pretty soon.

'Compared with the AV-8A, it's all up except the workload. Range up, payload up, accuracy up, maneuverability up, workload down. When we were out at Yuma we were fragged [detailed] to do a wing escort of a helicopter formation, with us and a bunch of AV-8As flying a top cover weave over these CH-53s and stuff. Real fuel-thirsty work. Well, after about 45 minutes the As bingoed out for fuel and I had another 15–20 minutes on station, easily.

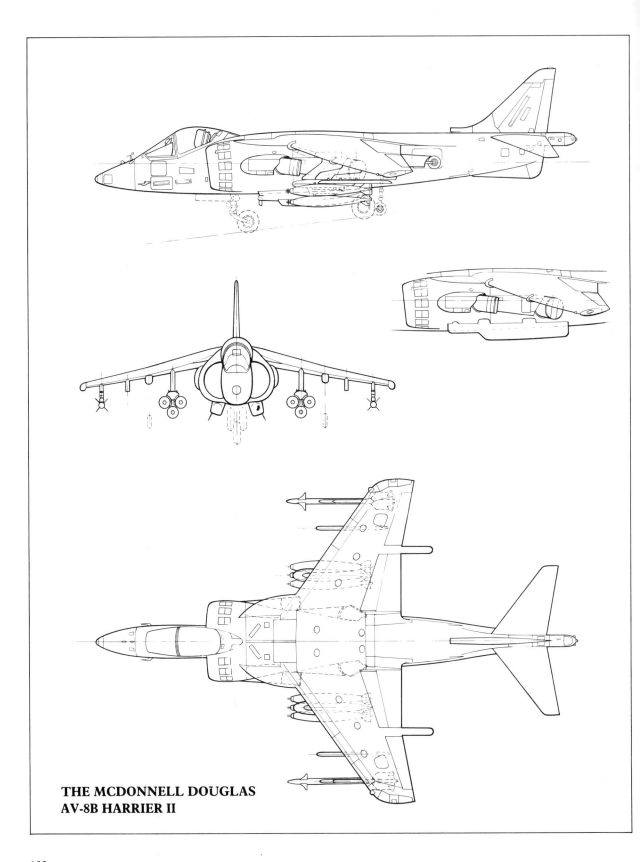

**THE MCDONNELL DOUGLAS
AV-8B HARRIER II**

'Another plus point is the INS computer. It says, "OK, dummy, this is what you've got, this is where we are and *this* is where you'll be when you run out of fuel." If I want to I can call up on the DDI [Digital Data Indicator] my best cruise profile, best altitude for range, all that back of book stuff right there, when I need it.

'This DDI on nav gives me the God's eye view of the world with me in the center. I can have tacan on it, INS information, time to go, distance to go, what's on the pylons, and engine data. The laser info will go on there, and the ALQ-162. And I can call down the HUD info to the DDI if the HUD goes unserviceable on me. It feels unusual flying HUD in DDI. I've done it a couple of times for practice, but it's good, it works. Really the HUD is good in itself – everything you want is there but not cluttered, the up-front radio selection, the HOTAS.

'You don't have to look inside this airplane's cockpit unless you're bored. The INS is very accurate. If we get more than three-quarters of a nautical mile error after a normal sortie, then I will have the guys look at it. I've got used to expecting it to get me there, and I don't mean a quarter mile either side. With this, the IP [Initial Point] comes up bang on the nose.

'The ARBS is outstanding. On an A-4 or F-4 squadron the old heads will get a CCIP [continuously computed impact point] bomb of about 50ft CEP [circular error probable] and the nuggets, the young guys, turn in CEPs of say 70–75ft, something like that. Now look at this. This is our squadron dive-bombing ladder. [The highest CEP was 58ft by a pilot with 125 hours on type. Most figures were in the late 'teens and early twenties, with a sprinkling of direct hits. High-time pilots had 187hrs on type.]

'OK, that's academic range work. In real life you've got SAMs, AAA, bad guys, to contend with. With the AV-8B I can use terrain masking to run in low. My accurate INS puts me on the IP, I pull and zoom, say to attack a SAM site, up high, roll in, drop on the SAMs before I get into the AAA range, then beat feet outa there, and d'you know what's really nice? I won't have to go back and do it again tomorrow because I missed – that *is* nice. All the time I'm in that attack the system is working for me.

'I don't need to worry about airspeed, wind velocity, angle of dive, or all that old stuff. I can use my guns and drop my bombs at the same time, give the guys shooting at *me* a hard time;

Early AV-8B on weapons trials.

The TAV-8B offers two-seat training to the US Marines.

The cockpit of an RAF Harrier GR.5. Unlike that of the AV-8B, it features a moving map display.

The McDonnell Douglas TAV-8B Harrier II.

that's nice, too! This aeroplane and ARBS puts the bomb exactly where you lock it – now if that isn't where the target is that's *your* fault. My worst bomb was a 150ft miss on a loft attack because *I* screwed up. When I don't, this sucker can loft in a 20ft bomb from three miles out.

'In ACM [Air Combat Maneuvering], well we haven't really gotten into that yet, but what we have done leaves no doubt in my mind that nobody sits in my six unless I want him there. We've done some tail chases, [but] we don't have the DRS yet. It'll be retrofitted later so we

go up to 17.6 alpha, where we get the first tones (audio warning). Now forget flaps and forget nozzles and forget that fancy viffing talk. This bird will *turn*, just because of that big wing and the lerxes (leading edge root extensions): you can really pull on it, and no one should be able to out-turn you, even conventionally. If they do, then you still can viff or drop some flap. It'll give your F-15 driver fits, guaranteed grade A fits.

'The cockpit visibility is tremendous. You can see down below, over the nose, see your pylons, fin, even the tailplane without strain-

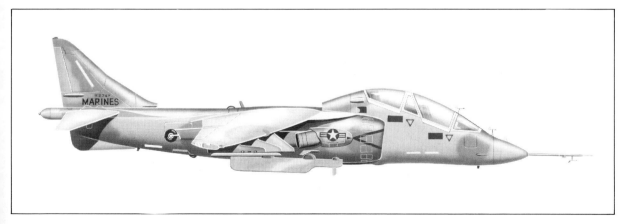

The larger wing of the
Harrier II is clearly
evident in this view.

ing. You can check your wingman's six is clear
with a quick glance rather than straining round
like in the AV-8A. It's a very aggressive airplane
in the defensive mode. We've got teeth, especially if the other guy wants to get into a furball.
That gun is good, extremely accurate and
extremely punchy. I'm leaving the guns on my
aircraft all the time. So long as the Marines give
me bullets to put in 'em, they stay on. With
other airplanes the guns are draggy, but these
aren't.

'The refueling probe only weighs 102lb, so
that's staying on my aircraft too. Air-to-air
refueling is a piece of cake in the B. Let's be fair,
it's not hard in the A either, but with that big
wing and auto stab it's really so easy in the B,
just plug in and fill up, no sweat at all. But don't
forget, this airplane will go for an hour at 420kt
at low level with internal fuel only.

'In the landing pattern in an AV-8A the pilot
has no spare capacity. He's constantly watching
his AoA, wind on nose, and engine parameters,
and he loses wing lift at, say, 90kt. In the AV-8B
at half weight you can fly right down to 50kt
with 60 degree nozzle. And it's so stable, like it's
on rails. The SAS has so much authority that
you go straight up or down. Not like in the AV-
8A, where if the pilot is tight on the stick you
can see all the wobbles. The AV-8B does not
wobble around, and you'll drop the last six feet
then dance around on the gear.

'For a rolling vertical landing in a cross-wind,
say 100kt with 30kt of wind at 35 degrees off the
nose, you have to be sure you kick off *all* the
drift before you touch down. In the AV-8A, the
outriggers would give you a bit of leeway and
pull you round straight. With the B, the outriggers are closer to the fuselage so it won't pull
you round, and so if you are not straight it gets a
bit squirley. These carbon brakes take a bit of
getting used to, too. They're extremely positive.
Think 'brake' and you stop, which can be rough
on the tyres.

'You can tell I'm enthusiastic, I suppose, but
I want a moving map display. The system we
have is good, but I don't want to run into a hill
because the FAC [Forward Air Controller]
forgets to tell me it's there. No, I want a moving
map display with nice contours on it. At present
I carry maps, at least they give us lots of space to
stash things in around the cockpit.

'You can tell my RAF friends that they'll love
the Harrier GR.5 (especially since they've got
six Sidewinder stations *and* my moving map).
This is a damn good airplane. I'm confident I
can send out my young kids on the squadron to
do real close work without killing our own
troops, and I'm also convinced that the AV-8B
will have a much lower accident rate than the
AV-8A suffered. I'm not worried about my
young kids in the circuit or on the boat. All they
have to do is not fly into a mountain or something. The first RAF squadron commander with
GR.5 is going to be a very happy man.'

The Royal Air Force's long experience of operating the Harrier in the tactical and battlefield roles has enabled it to develop the inherent flexibility of the aircraft, notably its capability to operate off-base from small, semi-prepared areas with minimal support, which allows it to be deployed to the maximum tactical advantage. In the naval environment, similar consideration has been given to developing this capability of the Harrier. While it is obvious that deployment of the Harrier at sea must be restricted by its need to be based upon a vessel of some description, there are a number of developments which have a particular potential for using the aircraft's flexibility to the fullest degree.

This again points to a fundamental consideration when assessing the true measure of any weapon system, be it aircraft, warship or tank: that, regardless of its success in its original role, a truly great weapon is one whose basic characteristics are capable of being developed to meet the evolving demands of warfare. In this respect, the Harrier and Sea Harrier demonstrate undeniable qualifications.

In the course of the Falklands campaign, a number of developments were tried out which will become an integral part of Harrier/Sea Harrier naval operations in the future, among the most important of which was the use of merchant ships to augment the theatre tactical air power capacity. *Atlantic Conveyor* became the best-known of these ships. A container/ro-ro (roll-on/roll-off) ship, *Atlantic Conveyor* was used as a Harrier transport vessel. She was converted, in only three days, to carry eight Sea Harrier FRS.1s and six Harrier GR.3s to the Fleet in the South Atlantic, in addition to helicopters and other vital stores and equipment. Another such vessel which acted as a Harrier 'garage ship' was the *Contender Bezant*, while the conversion of *Astronomer*, with a hangar for four aircraft, had almost been completed when the conflict ended. *Astronomer* was subsequently commissioned into the Royal Fleet Auxiliary as RFA *Reliant*.

A year after the Falklands War, a benign gremlin took a hand and put the Sea Harrier's capabilities in the news again – but in very different circumstances. On 6 June 1973, Lt. Ian Watson RN provided the world with an amazing example of the aircraft's ability to land virtually anywhere. In this case, with particular pertinence, the site was the deck of a small freighter, *Alraigo*, whose captain and crew were, moreover, quite unprepared for what was about to descend on them.

'THE ALRAIGO KID'

The day started normally for Lt. Watson, who was serving with No. 801 Squadron aboard HMS *Illustrious*. The carrier had recently left Lisbon to take part in the NATO Exercise 'Jolly Roger', but the decision was made en route first to take part in an exercise to locate and simulate an air strike against the French aircraft carrier *Foch*.

The first pair of Sea Harriers launched from the *Illustrious* to search for, locate and attack *Foch* returned to their parent ship with their mission unfulfilled, and Watson was detailed to fly one of a second pair to search for her. He and the other pilot were briefed in *Illustrious*' operations centre and assigned their pre-planned search area. The mission involved a hi-lo-hi sortie profile to avoid radar detection on the outward leg.

Watson himself told the story as follows:

'After launch from the carrier's flight deck, we left the ship on a northbound heading, flying low level at about 200 feet until we were approximately 100 nautical miles from *Illustrious*. After arriving at the pre-designated point we split up to search different sectors, thereby increasing the chances of locating the *Foch*. I turned on to a heading of 090 and climbed up to 30,000 feet to conserve fuel, and continued for about 130 miles on this leg before turning north for the next leg of the triangular-shaped search pattern. There was still no sign of the French carrier, and in fact since launch I had seen only a couple of ships on the outward leg. It was rather unnerving really, knowing one was out there alone, surrounded by sea and sky.

'After completing the next sector of the search pattern, the problems began when I selected my destination (*Illustrious*) on the NavHARS (Navigation and Heading Reference System), which gave me spurious information for my return to the ship. So I had no alternative but to continue on dead reckoning navigation. After this northerly leg, I had turned left and assumed my course for position Bravo Bravo – the low level position to be at for the return to the *Illustrious*. I set off back to the ship on the assumed course, which was a southerly heading. At a point I estimated to be about 40 nautical miles from the carrier I turned on the Blue Fox radar – nothing was coming up on the screen. The radar was working, but nothing was showing. I climbed to 5,000 feet and called on the main radio, which proved unserviceable. The standby set also didn't work.

'I searched for *Illustrious* in a north-south direction for 10–15 minutes at high level. By this time I was getting rather low on fuel, though the situation was not yet critical – I think I had about 2,000lb left. I decided that the chance of finding *Illustrious* was slim and therefore chose to fly east towards the shipping lanes so that, on abandoning the aircraft, I would be

picked up quickly. I did not have enough fuel to make landfall.

'To reduce the drag on the aircraft, I jettisoned the large 100-gallon drop tanks which were empty and carried on, though by now the fuel state was really beginning to cause me some concern as I was getting down to 600–700lb, the normal minimum landing allowance being 1,000lb. Fortunately I had kept my radar on, and I spotted a contact on the screen at a range of about 60 nautical miles. I turned towards it and went into a cruise descent, passing through the cloud base at about 3,000 feet and spotting the contact which was about 30 degrees off to the right. It turned out to be a small freighter of about 3,500 tons.

'Approaching the ship – the *Alraigo* – I flew down her port side first to attract the attention of the crew prior to ejecting so that I would be picked up quickly. As I passed the freighter and turned starboard, a thought developed that the deck size between the bridge and central derrick looked the same size as one of the pads I had used at RAF Wittering on my conversion course. Having carried out a reconnaissance, albeit a somewhat brief one, I completed a right-hand orbit around the ship to return to her port side, completing landing checks. I then brought the Sea Harrier into the hover parallel to and midway between the bridge and the derrick. Unlike the speculation that appeared in the media at the time of the event, I did not wave, signal or call on the radio to the *Alraigo*'s captain prior to the landing.

'Once in a suitable hovering position, I transitioned across the ship at a height of about twenty feet above her deck level. The fuel state at this time was extremely low, so without further ado I carried out a vertical landing on the containers secured to her main deck. As soon as I had landed, I felt the aircraft slipping backwards – the nosewheel had touched down but the main twin-wheeled undercarriage had just missed the edge of the containers. Consequently, the aircraft immediately began to adopt a tail down/nose up position, and I retracted the undercarriage and secured the engine. Immediately after the aircraft started to slide back it came to a halt, so the thought of ejecting at that point did not enter my mind.

'The aircraft came to rest on the gun pods (which did not have guns fitted), the nose leg (which had failed to retract) and the two outboard wing pylons. I vacated the aircraft as

soon as it stopped moving, putting the safety pins back into the Martin-Baker seat. An inert acquisition [practice] Sidewinder missile on the starboard outer weapon pylon also came into contact with the containers. The head of the missile broke off and came to rest on the ship's starboard main deck catwalk.

'Now all I had to do was face the captain and crew and explain why a Navy fixed-wing jet had just hitched a ride on their rather small ship. A welcoming committee of about four men was coming along the catwalk and they took me up to the bridge to meet the *Alraigo*'s captain. Once I had assured them I was not carrying any live armament and the aircraft was safe, I asked to use the marine radio to try to contact HMS *Illustrious* and inform them of my predicament and whereabouts, but on this occasion I was denied permission to do so. However, by about 1 or 2am the following morning, I was in contact with the British Embassy in Madrid and in turn they informed the carrier via London as to my whereabouts.

'Once we had dealt with the important formalities, I was able to settle down a bit and try to come to terms with my surroundings. I was treated very hospitably by the *Alraigo*'s

Sub-Lt. Watson reunited at last with ZA176 at RNAS Yeovilton. The aircraft was subsequently allocated to No. 899 Naval Air Squadron. (Royal Navy)

crew who provided me with some clothes, an en-suite cabin, cigarettes and drinks. In the meantime the crew, with my assistance, had managed to shackle the aircraft to lashing points on the containers and deck to secure it from further movement.'

On Thursday 9 June, the *Alraigo* docked at Santa Cruz in Tenerife, where Watson was interviewed by the Spanish port authorities prior to debriefing by a Royal Navy party and the subsequent inevitable press conference. The following morning, he was flown to Madrid and then back to the United Kingdom for a much-needed break. After only a short while ashore he was flown from RNAS Culdrose in a Grumman C-2 on-board delivery aircraft to the US carrier *John F. Kennedy*, whose captain had asked to meet him. A US Navy helicopter took him back

to *Illustrious*, which was nearby. He was airborne in a Sea Harrier again that afternoon.

As far as Watson's 'own' Sea Harrier – ZA176 – was concerned, the Royal Navy party sent out to recover it from the *Alraigo*'s deck decided that it would be impracticable to remove the wing, so the aircraft was craned off in one piece. Rather than lift the aircraft back to the United Kingdom by air, it was put on board the British Petroleum tanker *British Tay* and shipped to Portland, where it was offloaded. Still complete with its wing, ZA176 made the last part of its journey to RNAS Yeovilton on a low-loader. When the aircraft was fully inspected, there was no fuel aboard it at all.

Lt. Watson subsequently departed on a seven-month overseas cruise to the Far East and Australia on board HMS *Invincible* with No. 801 Squadron. The *Alraigo*'s owners and crew

were awarded £500,000 for their part in the salvage operation, and, after being fully stripped down and overhauled, ZA176 was allocated to No. 899 Headquarters and Training Squadron, RNAS Yeovilton.

SCADS

Studies have been going on in the United Kingdom and in the United States since the mid-1970s into the use of commercial container ships as auxiliary helicopter and aircraft carriers. The big modern container ship offers an ideal basic configuration – a long unobstructed top deck and high speed, usually in excess of 20kts. With very little penalty to the peacetime use of such a ship, a runway can be provided for the aircraft by fitting rapidly rigged decking, supported by the top layer of containers. Such a ship, in time of war, could augment a fleet's carrier force at a fraction of the cost of a standard flat top, and that conversion could be carried out at extremely short notice.

This analysis was at least partly proved when *Atlantic Conveyor* was chosen as a Harrier transport ship. She differed from the total concept in that she did not feature a full-length runway nor did she have a ski-jump as would have been the case with a complete conversion (for which there was simply insufficient time in April 1982), but she did prove the approach to be sound and practical. Her destruction by an Exocet surface-to-air missile, however, was in part attributable to her having no means of defending herself.

Spurred on by the use of merchant ships as 'Harrier carriers' during the Falklands campaign, British Aerospace completed the initial study of a Shipborne Containerized Air Defence System (SCADS). The concept is based on the containerization of several military systems – Sea Harrier support facilities, Seawolf antimissile system(s) (particularly the vertical-launch lightweight version), air defence/surveillance radar, active missile countermeasures and, if required, ASW helicopter support. Royal Engineers Medium Girder Bridge elements are the basic units used for the Harrier runway and ski-jump. The containerized systems would be suitable for carriage on a variety of commercial container ships, and the full potential of the Harrier could be realized using those ships able to provide a 120m take-off run.

A total of 233 20ft ISO containers would be needed for a full installation. These would include command and control facilities, accommodation units for 31 officers and 159 ratings, self-contained power and water supplies and logistic support for about 30 days' operation at sea. The requirements would be: aircraft support, 77 containers; weapons systems, 16; personnel support, 62; and general support, 78.

The study shows that the ship could be rigged and ready to proceed to sea after about two days' work. For an investment which amounts to a small fraction of that required for an equivalent warship, it is possible to provide integral combat airpower at sea with a task force or convoy in circumstances where existing fighting ships are to be committed elsewhere.

ROLES

A ship fitted with SCADS equipment would form a higly effective unit for reconnaissance, defensive or offensive operations. The primary role of a SCADS ship is area air defence, supplementing the existing capability of the force with which it will be operating. The concept is planned on the basis of 30 days' autonomous, unreplenished operation, with a unit of six Sea Harriers and two AEW (airborne early warning) helicopters such as the Sea King. The flexibility of the container-based system allows the mix of Harriers and helicopters to be changed according to role priorities. Provision is made for logistic support of the aircraft for up to six sorties per day and assumes a maximum flying rate of some 50 hours per aircraft within the 30-day operational period. This is typical of the flying rate achieved during the Falklands campaign. A mission may readily be extended by replenishment at sea (RAS) of fuel and other stores from a supply ship, or by helicopter replenishment (VERTREP) via the flight deck.

Operating from a 400ft runway and a 12° ski-jump, which would be provided on a typical SCADS ship, Sea Harrier is able to launch at a weight of 23,000lb. This assumes a short-lift, wet take-off at ISA plus 15°C. At this weight, and armed with air-to-air missiles and 30mm guns in its primary role of area air defence, the Sea Harrier is capable of accomplishing high-level interceptions – out to some 400nm under initial direction from some other source (surface ship or AEW aircraft) or out to approximately 100nm for targets detected by the SCADS radar. Low-flying targets detected by an AEW aircraft can be intercepted out to some 350nm from the ship.

Although the principal role of SCADS is long-

Ian Watson's Sea Harrier stripped down so that a full inspection of all component parts can be carried out. This work was undertaken at the Royal Naval Air Station at Yeovilton by Fleet Air Arm maintainance engineers. (Royal Navy)

range air defence, Seawolf missiles and Shield decoy systems provide a self-defence capability and help with the overall defence of the entire force. The point defence provided by these systems allows the SCADS ship to operate confidently within areas of tension or conflict, and the provision of a surveillance and command system makes it highly effective as a warship. By its nature, SCADS is a highly flexible, simple and mobile system. Therefore, although SCADS includes a command centre for the co-ordination of its own systems, it is not envisaged that the complex tactical command facilities of a flagship would be required. Consequently, control of the overall tactical situation would be carried out in another ship of the force, and appropriate information and commands would be passed on to SCADS by data link.

The absence of an immediate air threat would allow the reconnaissance role to be a natural function of the Sea Harrier and complementary to that of the AEW helicopter. In the reconnaissance role, the aircraft can, using its Blue Fox radar, probe a contact at a radius of 560nm from the force, and when flying a low-level reconnaissance and probe mission, an area of 28,000 square nautical miles can be surveyed in about 100 minutes.

Studies so far have been confined to examining the SCADS concept in the air defence, reconnaissance and surface strike roles. However, SCADS can be expanded to allow the aircraft to undertake the roles of anti-submarine warfare (ASW) and the close air support (CAS) of forces ashore. As with all V/STOL aircraft carriers, a SCADS ship can support an amphibious or land operation some hundreds of miles from a task force, and can also disembark aircraft to operate from a beach-head or at a convenient airfield ashore. Provision has been made within the concept for the storage of further armaments required to meet these roles.

SHIP CONVERSION

Speed of conversion of the ship from a mercantile to a military role at times of tension is a fundamental aim of the SCADS concept. A target of 48 hours is envisaged. Containerization provides a convenient method of handling the equipment, and speed of installation is achieved by considering the ship as a basic flat-topped hull on to which the SCADS equipment is loaded in the simplest possible way. The SCADS elements are arranged to minimize the number of commercial containers that have to be removed, and all equipment is fitted above the hatch covers at weather-deck level, allowing containers below this level to remain undisturbed. Any dependence on the existing facilities of the ship is avoided, with the exception of the firemains, all equipment being self-sufficient in power supplies and support. As well as speeding the conversion process, this enables the individual elements of SCADS to be used ashore as separate systems if required. The only permanent modifications required are the strengthening of the radar mast and the addition of a small number of attachment points which are used to secure the flight deck, ski-jump and some elements of the weapon systems. No major structural changes are required. Because of the simplicity of the modifications, the cost of preparation is very low, and a large number of container ships of different designs can therefore be modified as SCADS-designated ships. This maximizes the speed of response in times of tension and increases flexibility by ensuring that there is always a suitable ship within easy reach of a convenient port at which the SCADS equipment can be mobilized.

The ship on which the SCADS study is based is typical of container ships currently operating worldwide in both configuration and length – a British Shipbuilders design of 700ft overall length, 108ft beam and 36,000 tonnes deadweight, with a container capacity of 2,000teu (20ft equivalent units). However, the SCADS concept is equally applicable to other designs and sizes of container ship. The fundamental requirement is a long, uninterrupted length of forward deck for conversion into a flight deck. Once a ship is identified as SCADS-capable, a simple layout study would be carried out to determine the optimum arrangement of equipment. When this is complete, the number and type of specialist containers required, the routing of the power, signal and fluid lines, and any modifications to the ship can be defined.

In the typical SCADS ship, the support facilities for men and equipment are housed in the containers across which the flight deck and helideck are laid. In order to make maximum use of the available deck area, the runway and ski-jump are offset to the port side of the ship. A hangar suitable for the servicing of two aircraft occupies the forward end of the starboard side of the deck, the stack of containers forming the forward wall of the hangar accommodates the Seawolf and Shield systems, workshops and various stores, and the remaining deck area is utilized for aircraft parking at readiness and for minor servicing. This arrangement obviates the need for an aircraft lift and provides the maximum operational area for the aircraft. Dependent upon the configuration of the host vessel, this layout provides a runway 400ft long by 45ft wide, terminating in a 12° ski-jump and allowing the vertical landing spot to be positioned close to the centre of the ship. The helideck is positioned aft of the superstructure and allows a helicopter to approach from either side of the ship. A hangar to accommodate one Sea King is provided immediately forward of the helideck.

Under the aircraft flight deck, the arrangement of containers and their use is dictated to some extent by aircraft operations. As the main parking and operational preparation area for the aircraft occupies the aft section of the flight deck, the fuel storage is situated below this area for convenience and to reduce pump power requirements, but the area beneath the vertical landing spot is kept clear of combustible or explosive stores in order to minimize the possibility of secondary fires and damage in the event of a landing accident. The magazine containers are therefore sited forward of this area.

A bomb lift with a platform 18ft long by 7½ft wide is provided to transport armaments and other stores between the lower deck and the flight deck, and an area for weapons preparation runs athwartships from the bomb lift. The remaining area below the flight deck is allocated to additional workshops and stores, water generation, accommodation for ratings, sanitation, power generation and other incidental personnel support facilities. Officers' accommodation and sanitation facilities, galley, dining area, food and domestic stores and additional generators are provided below the helicopter flight deck.

CLOSE-IN DEFENCE

While the combination of Sea Harrier and Sea King provides the offensive element of SCADS, the system also has a formidable close-in air defence capability. This comprises double-

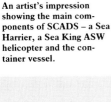

An artist's impression showing the main components of SCADS – a Sea Harrier, a Sea King ASW helicopter and the container vessel.

headed Seawolf missile installations and four Shield anti-ship missile decoy systems, both giving 360° coverage, and the AWS-5 surveillance and air traffic control radar. The British Aerospace Lightweight Seawolf is the only missile system available which provides effective defence against current and projected anti-ship missile threats, including sea-skimming missiles. Developed from the successfully combat-proven GWS-25 system in service with the Royal Navy on *Leander* and *Broadsword* Class frigates, Lightweight Seawolf is effective by day or night in all weathers against aircraft and very small, high-speed, manoeuvring targets. Its fully automatic operation and short reaction time, combined with a supersonic and very agile missile, ensure a high lethality, giving an improved level of ship survivability. Low mass, low maintenance requirements and a simple launcher based on existing equipment results in low initial and through-life costs.

For installation on a SCADS vessel, each major Lightweight Seawolf element is installed in its own standard ISO container. The testing and commissioning of the system can, therefore, be largely completed in the factory prior to installation on board ship, and, because container modules may be rapidly exchanged, a SCADS vessel is unlikely to be delayed in port because of weapon system servicing.

The new system uses a lightweight tracking and guidance system and a four-barrel launcher based on that designed for the Seacat, which is in service with many navies worldwide. A choice of two tracking and guidance systems is available, both of which are designed specifically to complement the performance of the Seawolf missile. The radars are of the narrow band, dual-frequency, differential tracking type, with significant improvements in low-level tracking accuracy, clutter rejection, resistance to jamming and reduction of multi-path effects. The lightweight barrels of the launcher also serve as both transportation and storage units, permitting the Seawolf missiles to be treated as rounds of ammunition during their life on board – an important factor in a SCADS configuration. As an alternative to the four-barrel launcher, a vertical-launch version of Seawolf is being developed, providing increased range, coverage and availability whilst being easily adaptable to containerization.

In operation, the lightweight radar provides tracking of both the target and the Seawolf missile. The missile is controlled throughout its flight by a microwave command link, guidance calculations being carried out on board ship so that a minimum of electronic equipment is carried on the missile. The cost per round is thereby reduced and reliability is enhanced. All operational functions of the system are completely automatic. System activities are normally only monitored by the operator, but provision has been made for manual control to be exercised when desired. A double-headed radar system as proposed for SCADS will provide all-round coverage and two independent channels of fire. This, together with the availability of salvo firing, maximizes the probability of defeating any attack.

While Seawolf assures close-in air defence, the Plessey Shield system provides passive protection for the SCADS ship from anti-ship missiles by the deployment of chaff and infra-red decoys. The system is made up of standard modules from the Shield range to provide launchers, control system and decoy rockets. The crossed-barrel launchers each comprise a simple, fixed base supporting two modules of three barrels at a fixed elevation of 30° and at an angular difference of 80° to each other. This assembly is then mounted on an ISO container along with a ready-use locker for the decoy rounds. The SCADS ship would have four of these containers, sited two on the bow and two on the stern, thereby giving all-round coverage against missile attack. The control system comprises a single command module, a launcher control module per pair of launchers and a loader switch per launcher. The Shield decoy rockets have been developed with an inventory of different decoy ammunition, including infra-red. The decoy most appropriate to the SCADS ship is a medium-range chaff rocket for use in the distraction mode of operation.

The radar chosen for the SCADS concept is the Plessey AWS-5, because of its ability to provide comprehensive surveillance facilities for both aircraft control and target indication. The AWS-5 achieves this flexibility by a number of special features in the radar's design. These include E/F-band transmissions for good medium/long range performance in extreme environmental conditions, separate high and low antenna beams providing near-hemispherical coverage and the earliest possible detection of high-diving and sea-skimming missiles, and two rotation rates which provide combined search and target indication information from a single radar system. Frequency-agile operation also

maintains detection performance during severe jamming and improves range performance in normal conditions. Pulse-to-pulse agility over a wide frequency band, and a separate frequency programme for the two beams, further enhance the ECCM (electronic counter-countermeasures) capability.

SKYHOOK

Another potentially valuable future application for the Sea Harrier is SkyHook. Developed jointly by British Aerospace and Dowty Boulton Paul, the concept involves the operation of V/STOL aircraft from small ships in conditions up to Sea State 6. It has already been shown that existing Sea Harriers, with only minimum modifications, can carry out many missions not possible by any other means with the use of this concept; in addition, aircraft developments already in the pipeline or under study could lead

to performances competitive with those currently possible from ski-jump equipped vessels.

SkyHook consists essentially of a crane which is capable of capturing a Harrier in the hover and placing it on or below deck. The lock-on mechanism is space-stabilized, allowing the ship considerable sea motion yet providing a stable platform for capture to be achieved. The pilot's task is to formate on a similarly space-stabilized hover sight which will guide him into the contact 'window', the actual capture being achieved by sensors locating the aircraft which hydraulically extend a lock-on jack to contact the aircraft's pick-up probe. The aircraft portion consists of a mast located closely above the centre of gravity. Once lock-on is achieved, the aircraft is pulled up and firmly docked on to pads. The SkyHook then swings inboard, progressively becoming ship-stabilized, allowing the aircraft to be placed on to a re-arming

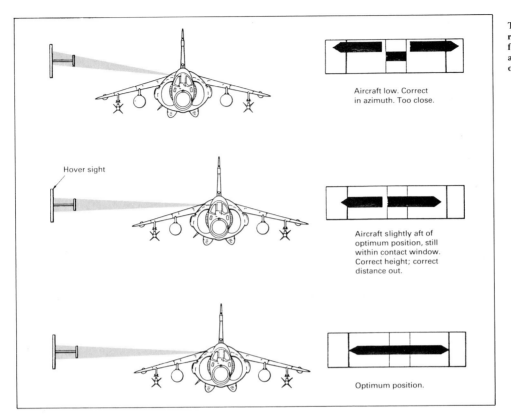

The SkyHook system requires the pilot to formate on the hover sight, aiming to align the arrows on the marker.

Aircraft low. Correct in azimuth. Too close.

Hover sight

Aircraft slightly aft of optimum position, still within contact window. Correct height; correct distance out.

Optimum position.

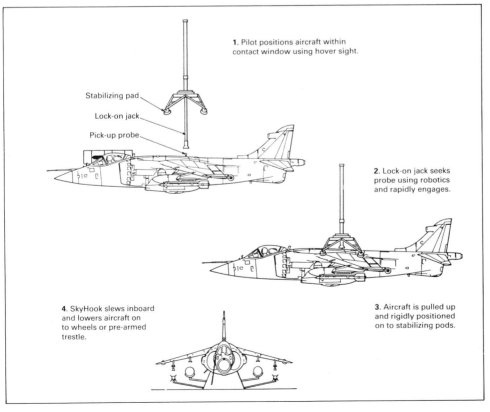

SkyHook capture sequence.

1. Pilot positions aircraft within contact window using hover sight.

Stabilizing pad

Lock-on jack

Pick-up probe

2. Lock-on jack seeks probe using robotics and rapidly engages.

4. SkyHook slews inboard and lowers aircraft on to wheels or pre-armed trestle.

3. Aircraft is pulled up and rigidly positioned on to stabilizing pods.

146

trestle or, on its wheels, on to the deck. If desired, the entire sequence of placing the aircraft on board may be carried out automatically. Launching the aircraft calls for the reverse procedure.

The space-stabilized crane is designed to operate in most sea conditions, although ship motion will depend on the type of vessel employed. Space-stabilization is achieved using a combination of inertial systems, computers and triple redundant control techniques derived from aviation systems experience. For the larger air-capable ships, it is proposed to use two SkyHooks both for quicker launching and recovery and to provide redundancy. The crane system can be designed to replenish the aircraft with fuel and water without its having to be recovered to the deck. Communication with the pilot is via a telebrief system.

AIRCRAFT OPERATION

To position the aircraft before lock-on, the pilot formates on a hover sight, which can be used day or night. The hover sight is attached to the lock-on mechanism and is therefore similarly space-stabilized. Using parallax, it provides the pilot with all the information required to bring his aircraft into the correct position for lock-on to be achieved. A display of lights indicates to the pilot the various stages of launching and recovery.

The SkyHook is initially extended from its stowed position on deck ready to receive the Harrier. The pilot commences a decelerating transition into the hover, aiming to come alongside the ship. When thus positioned, he concentrates on the hover sight and places the aircraft in the contact 'window', a 10ft cube, using standard hovering techniques. Once the aircraft is in position, lock-on can be achieved as soon as the optical system has acquired the aircraft. The system measures both angle and distance to the pick-up probe and automatically guides the lock-on jack, the latter being able to lock on to the aircraft anywhere within the window. The pilot continues to hover the aircraft, lock-on being indicated to him by either a series of lights, or radio, or both. When initial lock-on has taken place, the pilot reduces power by 5–10 per cent NF whilst still controlling the aircraft in three axes. The lock-on jack is then programmed to pull the aircraft on to the docking pads, thus rigidly capturing the aircraft.

If the aircraft is only to be fluid-replenished, the engine is allowed to idle whilst fuel and water transfer takes place. If the aircraft is to be re-armed, the pilot shuts down the engine after capture and the SkyHook swings inboard. Space stabilization gives way to ship stabilization, and the aircraft is lowered to the deck access area. The aircraft's trestle, which has been pre-armed, is positioned to receive the aircraft, and once lowered on to the trestle the aircraft is secured, electrical supplies are connected and re-arming is commenced.

With the rapid turn-round completed, the aircraft is ready for launch. The hangar access is opened and the SkyHook is programmed once again to lock on to the aircraft. When the lock is achieved, the trestle releases the aircraft and the SkyHook lifts the aircraft clear of the hangar. The device changes from ship-stabilization to space-stabilization when clear of ship obstructions, and the pilot starts the engine and commences his final cockpit checks. The aircraft is now ready for launch, the pilot receiving his final instructions through the telebrief system.

The pilot slowly increases engine rpm with the nozzles down in order to control the aircraft as the lock-on jack extends downwards, clear of the lock-on pads, a process which takes some ten seconds. The aircraft is now clear to disconnect, and with the green lights flashing on the lock-on board the pilot can slowly open up to full power. As soon as the lock-on jack senses an up-load, it will withdraw in less than one second. The aircraft is now in a free air hover, ready to move sideways and then transition ahead.

Aircraft operation on a conventional aircraft carrier can be extremely manpower-intensive, critical in terms of space required for safety and operationally very difficult in heavy sea states, and considerable savings in manpower and space can be achieved by mechanically handling the aircraft and weapons – a particularly important consideration in high sea states aboard a much smaller ship. The need for a SkyHook is, therefore, just as vital on deck as it is for assisting the aircraft from the hover to the deck.

Once the aircraft is below deck and finally secured on its trestle, it is possible to move it quickly and precisely to its parking position. It is this accurate positioning that allows many more aircraft to be parked below deck in a confined space. The size of the hangar, and the flight deck above it, is of course a matter of

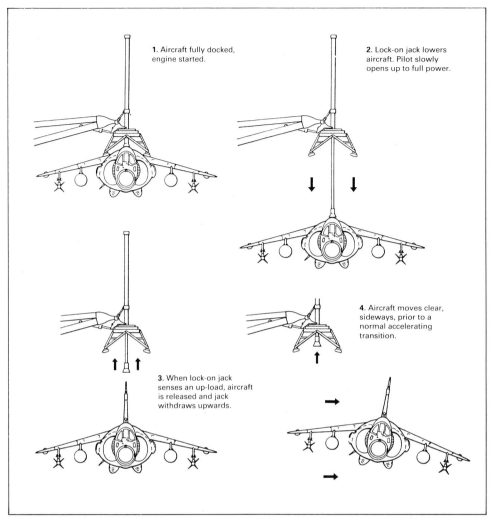

1. Aircraft fully docked, engine started.

2. Lock-on jack lowers aircraft. Pilot slowly opens up to full power.

3. When lock-on jack senses an up-load, aircraft is released and jack withdraws upwards.

4. Aircraft moves clear, sideways, prior to a normal accelerating transition.

SkyHook designed motion capacity.

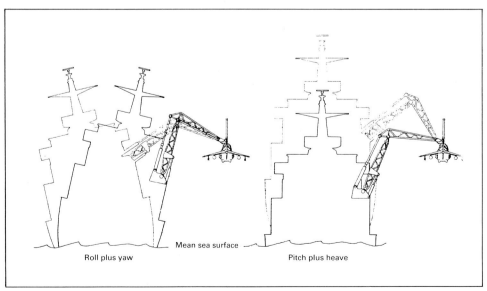

Mean sea surface

Roll plus yaw

Pitch plus heave

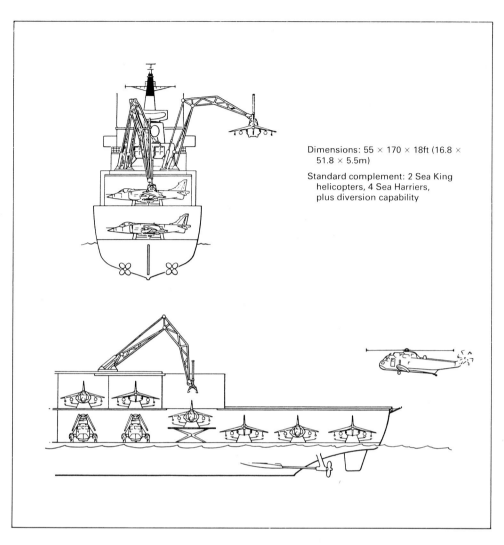

Dimensions: 55 × 170 × 18ft (16.8 × 51.8 × 5.5m)

Standard complement: 2 Sea King helicopters, 4 Sea Harriers, plus diversion capability

choice, depending on the ship, its tasks and the number of Harriers carried.

The SkyHook concept depends upon the ability of the pilot to position the aircraft within the contact window, and as the pilot's task is a combination of formation flying and hovering, BAe decided to carry out a short flight trial. The hover sight was mounted on the end of a hydraulic turntable used by British Fire Brigades and adjusted to give a horizontal distance of 30ft from board to pilot's eye, and the platform was raised to a height of 50ft. Three pilots participated in the trial, flying two types of Harrier, and proved conclusively that:

1. Formating in the hover was easy.

2. The horizontal distance of 30ft could comfortably be reduced to 25ft.

3. Positioning cues from the hover board were excellent.

4. Position accuracy within ±2ft was achieved over periods measured in tens of seconds, making the contact window of 10ft × 10ft × 10ft generous.

5. Aircraft relative velocity within the contact window was less than 1fs.

The exercise was completed with and without the use of autostabilization systems. The weather at the time of the trial was gusty, with wind speeds up to 25kts and 60° off aircraft axis.

CONCLUSIONS

The value of both SCADS and SkyHook is that they would make it possible to provide, at short notice, integral combat airpower at sea with a task force or convoy in circumstances where existing fighting ships were liable to be committed elsewhere. The SCADS concept is not restricted to the full range of offensive and

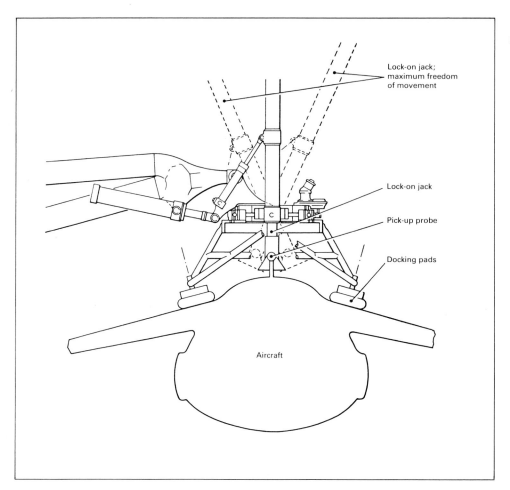

Lock-on jack;
maximum freedom
of movement

Lock-on jack

Pick-up probe

Docking pads

Aircraft

defensive systems described in this chapter; in fact, the Royal Navy has proceeded with the application of a SCADS arrangement for helicopters only, without Harriers or runway, in the container ship *Astronomer*, which is now operating as RFA *Reliant*. SkyHook, for its part, would not be confined in its application solely to new designs of ship: it could be applied retrospectively to destroyers, cruisers and naval auxiliaries, providing the Royal Navy with the ability to disperse and survive. The classic military virtues of flexibility and surprise, which V/STOL has so positively reintroduced to the concept of land-based tactical air power over the past twenty years, could be extended by SCADS and SkyHook across groups of ships on the high seas.

POSTSCRIPT: THE SEA HARRIER FRS.2

Benefiting from the outstanding success of the FRS.1 variant, the Sea Harrier design is at present being developed to take advantage of advances in military avionics and weapons technology. The result is the Sea Harrier FRS.2, which will offer the Royal Navy and potential overseas customers a greater capability in what is already a thoroughly proven aircraft.

The upgrade will considerably enhance the Sea Harrier's performance in the air defence, reconnaissance and surface attack roles. Central to the upgrade is the Ferranti Blue Vixen pulse-doppler, 'look-down shoot-down' radar, comprising a receiver-transmitter and flat-plate

An artist's impression of the Sea Harrier FRS.2.

antenna in a reshaped radome, a processor in the aft avionics bay, and a multi-purpose display in the cockpit. The radar will be used in conjunction with the Sea Harrier FRS.2's primary armament of four AIM-120 Advanced Medium Range Air-to-Air Missiles (AMRAAM), two of which will be carried on the outboard wing pylons and two under the fuselage in place of the 30mm guns. The cannon may be retained as an option, with either two AMRAAM or four Sidewinders on the outboard pylons.

The Hughes AIM-120 AMRAAM, which is intended to replace the heavier AIM-7 Sparrow MRAAM, offers a higher missile velocity, an

extended performance envelope and the ability to cope with threat systems likely to be in force over the next two decades. AIM-120 is an all-weather weapon designed to attack targets from any approach angle and at both visual and beyond visual ranges (BVR), and to engage multiple targets following a simultaneous launch. Before launch, the missile's mid-course inertial reference unit is given details of the target's position; once targets are within range, the launch aircraft is free to fire several rounds against one or more simultaneously.

Smiths Industries won design and development contracts in the FRS.2 programme for a digital air data computer, a modified HUD, twin multi-purpose displays, the weapon-aiming computer, a new missile control system for use with AMRAAM and a bus control for the 1553B digital databus. The pilot's control of the total weapons system is optimized with HOTAS (hands on throttle and stick) and UFC (up-front controller).

One important feature of the FRS.2 is provision for the Joint Tactical Information and Distribution System (JTIDS), which will give secure voice and data links and greatly enhance the aircraft's operational effectiveness in the highly complex communications environment of maritime warfare. The system replaces tacan. Marconi Space and Defence Systems are responsible for the FRS.2's new digital radar warning receiver (RWR), which will give a better capability against current and projected Warsaw Pact threats. The system warns the pilot of a threat, if it is locked on to him, and where exactly it is. In the absence of an active ECM system, as yet not planned for upgraded Sea Harriers, the RWR can trigger chaff dispensers.

At the end of 1987, two Sea Harrier FRS.1s were being modified to FRS.2 standard at Kingston. The first flight of the trials aircraft will be closely followed by the maiden flight of the first development FRS.2, followed a year or so later by the flight of the second development aircraft. Thirty of the Royal Navy's FRS.1s are scheduled for mid-life upgrade to FRS.2 standard, although the service is understood to be considering the purchase of additional new FRS.2s for delivery in the 1990s.

Operating from the Royal Navy's trio of aircraft carriers – *Invincible, Illustrious,* and *Ark Royal* – the Sea Harrier FRS.2 will ensure that the naval air squadrons retain an effective fixed-wing combat capability for a long time to come. And what is going on behind closed doors and under strict security wraps at British Aerospace's premises at Kingston in the realms of supersonic V/STOL research may one day result in yet another chapter of the Harrier saga.

	Harrier GR.3	Sea Harrier FRS.1	AV-8B Harrier II
Span	25ft 3in	25ft 3in	30ft 4in
Length overall	46ft 10in	47ft 7in	46ft 4in
Height	11ft 11in	12ft 2in	11ft 8in
Wing area	201 sq ft	201 sq ft	230 sq ft
Wheel track	22ft 0in	22ft 0in	17ft 0in
Max. take-off weight	25,200lb	26,200lb	29,750lb
Operating weight (empty)	13,535lb	13,444lb	14,647lb
Max. warload	8,000lb	8,500lb	9,200lb
VTO payload	5,000lb	5,000lb	7,900lb
Internal fuel	5,060lb	5,060lb	7,500lb
Max. external fuel	5,300lb	5,300lb	7,900lb
Powerplant	Pegasus 103	Pegasus 104	Pegasus 105
Engine thrust	21,500lb	21,500lb	21,750lb
Max. speed (sea level)	635kts	635kts	590kts
Max. speed (high altitude)	Mach 1.3	Mach 1.3	Mach 1.1
Ceiling	51,200ft	51,200ft	55,000ft
g limits	+7.8/–4.2	+7.8/–4.2	+7/–2.8
STO distance at max. load	1,000ft	1,000ft	1,150ft
Ferry range	1,850nm	2,000nm	2,060nm
Missions:			
Hi-lo-hi + 4,400lb	360nm	300nm (strike)	600nm
Lo-lo + 4,400lb	200nm	–	–
CAP for 1.5hrs	100nm	100nm	100nm/3hrs
Hi-hi	–	400nm (intercept)	–
First flight	August 1966	August 1978	November 1981

Note: Use of a 12° ski-jump increases launch weight by 2,500lb for the same take-off run, or reduces the take-off run by 50–60 per cent for the same weight. Mission figures are approximate.

INDEX